Get Writing!!

The Total Writing Program

Book 1 Grades 2-3
Sentences and Mechanical Control

Leif Fearn and Nancy Farnan

D1376662

This book is dedicated to the teachers who worked with us over the years, refining our profession's understanding of how to teach children and adolescents to write well. We particularly appreciate Suzanne Jackson, Ellen Phaneuf, and Diane Rocha.

These popular teacher resources and activity books are available from
ECS Learning Systems, Inc., for Grades Pre-K-6

AlphaCapers and Characters	Gr. Pre-K-1	2 Titles
Booklinks to American and World History	Gr. 4-8	12 Titles
The Bright Blue Thinking Books	Gr. 1-6	3 Titles
Building Language Power	Gr. 4-9	3 Titles
EnviroLearn™	Gr. K-5	5 Titles
Foundations for Writing	Gr. 2-8	2 Titles
Home Study Collection™	Gr. 1-6	18 Titles
Inkblots	Gr. K-6	3 Titles
The Little Red Writing Books	Gr. 1-6	3 Titles
Math Whiz Kids™	Gr. 3-5	4 Titles
Novel Extenders	Gr. 1-6	7 Titles
Once Upon A Time™ for Emerging Readers	Gr. K-2	10 Titles
Once Upon A Time™ (Books + Tapes)	Gr. K-2	10 Titles
The Picture Book Companion	Gr. K-3	3 Titles
Quick Thinking™	Gr. K-6	1 Title
Springboards for Reading	Gr. 3-6	2 Titles
Structures for Reading, Writing, Thinking	Gr. 4-9	4 Titles
Test Preparation Guides	Gr. 2-12	41 Titles
Thematic Units	Gr. K-8	23 Titles
Writing Warm-Ups™	Gr. K-6	2 Titles

To order, contact your local school supply store, or write:

ECS Learning Systems, Inc.
P.O. Box 791437
San Antonio, Texas 78279-1437

Editor: Shirley J. Durst
Cover/Page Layout: Kirstin Simpson
Book Design: Educational Media Services

ISBN 1-57022-194-4

Authors' Note

Leif Fearn's work with children and writing had its genesis many years ago when his sixth-grade students' fiction ended up as a full page of stories in the local newspaper. Later, in both the Southwest and Northwest, he had the opportunity to emphasize literacy development as a trainer of Head Start teachers and aides. His early applications of creative thinking to existing curriculum, however, eventually led to his and Nancy's conception of Balanced Writing instruction.

Nancy Farnan's teaching began with middle and secondary students in the Midwest. Early in her career, she experienced her students' learning to write as watching buds opening to full bloom—the changes were observable, tangible, and powerful. She was impressed by the power her students discovered as they became increasingly effective writers.

A little over a decade ago, Leif and Nancy began to use their experiences, along with those of several outstanding teachers and colleagues, to develop the concept of Balanced Writing instruction. For a decade they have worked with teachers in the Writing Institute for Teachers at San Diego State University, refining and adding to their conception of what a Balanced Writing program would look and sound like. They have authored and co-authored many books and articles on writing and regularly lead workshops to promote Balanced Writing instruction and literacy.

Today, Leif and Nancy teach at San Diego State University, where they share an office in the School of Teacher Education. As key figures in the development of Balanced Writing instruction, they have devoted their professional lives to literacy and the development of writing skills. Married, Leif and Nancy live in San Diego, California, where they meet regularly with the professional writers' community.

Contents

vi   About This Book

10   **Lesson 1—One Sentence at a Time**
Mentally constructing sentences and reading them aloud

18   **Lesson 2—Using Ideas to Make Sentences**
Thinking in main ideas at the sentence level

26   **Lesson 3—Main Ideas in Double Sentence Strings**
Mentally constructing, writing, and reading related sentences

34   **Lesson 4—Planning Words in Sentences**
Crafting single sentences based on letter cues

42   **Lesson 5—Writing Sentences with Capital Letters and End Marks**
Beginning sentences with capital letters and using appropriate end marks

50   **Lesson 6—Writing Sentences with Rhyming Words**
Producing rhyming words in response to teacher prompts

58   **Lesson 7—Combining Sentences to Make Meaning**
Combining two short sentences into one longer sentence, both orally and in writing

66   **Lesson 8—Writing Sentences with Commas in Series**
Thinking in and writing sentences that contain items in series

76   **Lesson 9—Writing is the Reason for Spelling**
Focusing attention on spelling words properly

86   **Lesson 10—Writing Sentences that Contain Nouns**
Thinking and writing in sentences that contain specified nouns

94 Lesson 11—Writing Sentences that Contain Verbs

Thinking in and writing sentences that contain specified nouns and verbs

104 Lesson 12—Writing Sentences that Contain Modifiers

Using adjectives and adverbs to enhance nouns and verbs in sentences

110 Appendix
Organizing for Long-Term Instruction

—Mission Statement
—Assessment
—Sample One-Year Calendar
—Sample One-Month Calendar
—Bibliography

About This Book

 ## The Get Writing!! Series

The **Get Writing!!** series is a comprehensive, teacher-friendly, Balanced Writing program for kindergarten through fifth grade.

Balanced Writing instruction was born in the late 1970s as Developmental Writing, an application of creative thinking skills to teaching and learning basic school skills and content (Fearn, 1976). Balanced Writing instruction focuses specific attention on balancing three components of writing associated with learning to write well:

1. The **CONTENT** of writing
   - Sentence thinking and writing
   - Thinking and writing in relationships between and among sentences
   - Thinking and writing in paragraphs
   - Progressive mastery of writing for various purposes across the genres
   - Progressive mastery of writing conventions
   - Assessment and editing

2. The **PROCESSES** involved in learning and writing
   - Written interactions between planning and drafting and between drafting and revision
   - Control of the cognitive devices of attention
   - Conceptualization
   - Application of specific creative thinking skills

3. The **TIME** demands for learning
   Ideally, practice in Balanced Writing instruction should be ten percent of the instructional week, or up to 100 to 150 clock minutes of instructional time per week.

 ## What's Inside This Book?

The lessons in **Get Writing!!** relate directly to every student in the room. They specify student writing behaviors, include multiple procedures for the assessment of writing, and describe, in the most explicit terms, what teachers and students can do to achieve specified objectives.

Get Writing!! Book 1, Grades 2-3, Sentences and Mechanical Control, is a Balanced Writing approach to teaching second- and third-grade students to think in and write effective sentences. Students learn to plan their sentences in response to teacher prompts, choosing nouns, verbs, and modifiers to express their main ideas. They then learn to mentally construct sentences, verbalize them, and write them on paper, while maintaining proper capitalization, punctuation, and spelling. Use *Get Writing!! Book 1 Grades 2-3, Sentences and Mechanical Control*, with *Get Writing!! Book 2, Paragraphs and Forms of Writing.*

   ©ECS Learning Systems, Inc., San Antonio, TX

Lesson Design

Each lesson in this book begins with Information for the Teacher and with a section of detailed instructions and examples for conducting the lesson. These examples include a synopsis of student/teacher dialogue based on actual sessions with children and adolescents. For identification purposes, the teacher's comments and questions are enclosed in quotations and the students' comments are enclosed in parentheses.

Each lesson also includes the following:
- Daily Writing Activities
- Applications of the Lesson Across the Curriculum
- Applications for English Language Learners
- Reproducible Language Activity Sheets for classroom use

As with any other skill, writing skills can be acquired at more than one level of sophistication. Thinking in sentences, for instance, is introduced in *Get Writing!! Kindergarten* and *Get Writing!! Grade 1*, applied to writing in *Get Writing!! Books 1* and *2 Grades 2-3*, and again in *Get Writing!! Books 1* and *2 Grades 4-5*. Certain activities are appropriate at any grade level. If students claim they "did this last year," they can be reminded that what they remember about writing from last year will give them a running start this year.

Hints for Supporting a Balanced Writing Program

- **Writing instruction should focus young writers' attention on creation (the thinking in writing) and on making the scribal part of writing as automatic as possible.** In writing, practice makes automatic, so some instructional processes should emphasize speed and quantity.

- **Remember: Practice makes permanent.** Every instance of writing, no matter the context, the reason, the audience, the genre, the authenticity—is an instance of practice. If we want good writing from our first-, fifth-, and tenth-graders, we have to ensure that they write well every time. Our piano teachers and football coaches have the right idea, but mere practice doesn't make perfect; perfect practice makes perfect.

- **In writing instruction, as in all instruction, certain basic principles of teaching and learning must not be compromised.** First, learners must understand what is being taught. They must understand what they are supposed to do, and how they are supposed to do it. Secondly, good instruction takes advantage of, and honors, the prior knowledge that learners bring to school. Third, because children have three options in the classroom (to approach, to avoid, or to ignore), good teachers make sure most of the children achieve nearly all of the time. This virtually precludes avoiding and ignoring.

Get Writing!!
Main Ideas in Sentences

- **Call activities by their right names and frame directions in the vocabulary of writing.**

  Example: "That's a sentence, Eric. Read it again. Everyone, listen to Eric's sentence."

- **Avoid complex definitions.** For example, if you want a complex sentence, it isn't necessary to define dependent and independent clauses and the relationship(s) between the two. Instead, prompt students to think of a sentence in which the first word is *although*. Then, direct them to listen to examples from other students in the room. Call attention to accurate models and reinforce.

- **Never give more time to write than young writers need.** If they are given five minutes, four will need six; if they are given six, three of the four will need seven. If they are given one minute, they'll think they can't do it, but most will. Everyone, novice and expert alike, can produce written language a whole lot faster, and better than they think they can. An important part of learning to write is experiencing our own ability to achieve.

- **All writers must take full responsibility for spelling accurately, but don't let students' inability to spell a word correctly interfere with writing their draft.** At this point, the message to students must be, "Spell as well as you can."

- **Everything in this book is about fluency, precision, quantity, and quality at the same time.** Getting it down on paper and getting it right are not opposites, and neither one compromises the other. Monitor students' writing by standing behind them as they read aloud.

  Example: "Put a comma right here, Cheryl. Boys and girls, remember that we always use commas when we write sentences that contain items in a series."

- **Avoid putting young writers in the position of having to live up to perfection.** Rather than saying, "That's the best paragraph in the world, Ramon," say, "That's a terrific paragraph, Ramon. Read it again."

- **Make sure that most of the writing students do is both oral and written (scribal).** Part of learning to write is establishing the sound of good writing.

  Example: "Read it again, Margo, and everyone listen to the sound of Margo's sentence."

Portfolios

A portfolio is a collection of work, often one's "Best Efforts." There is little or no reason for having writing portfolios in classrooms where children and young adolescents don't write much, but in classrooms where they do, they need a place to keep and organize their work.

Young writers write an enormous amount in this program. They write every day across content areas and through the genres, both collaboratively and alone. Youngsters who write this much need a place to collect, organize, and reflect upon their work. It is recommended that each student in this program keep and maintain a writing portfolio (Farnan and Fearn, 1994).

English Language Learners

Every lesson in the **Get Writing!!** series has a section describing applications for children who do not speak English as a native language. Our experience and research shows that the Balanced Writing instruction represented in this program is successful with non-native speakers of English. The oral language component of the program is embedded in every lesson and is especially important for these students whose native language is not English.

Application to Children and Young Adolescents with Special Needs

The first formal study of the impact of balanced writing instruction was conducted with learning disabled elementary school children (Prior, 1979). Focusing on developmental student performance tends to cut through the various "disabling" conditions. Given prior assessment of suitability to the skill level of the students, the activities in the **Get Writing!!** series are entirely appropriate for special needs youngsters.

Home Schoolers

Balanced writing instruction has been used successfully by home school parents for many years. It is linguistically rigorous and intellectually demanding. It can be handled on a whole class, small group, or individual basis. The procedures associated with each lesson in this book are clear and focus on the developmental performance of young writers. While no collection of instructional materials is appropriate for everyone under all circumstances, this program contains literacy activities that have been used under a vast array of circumstances, including the home school setting.

Get Writing!! Book 1 Grades 2-3   ©ECS Learning Systems, Inc., San Antonio, TX   ix

1 One Sentence at a Time

—The great American novel is written one sentence at a time.

 ## Information for the Teacher

To learn to write well, young writers must understand the idea of sentence as their entrée into writing grander messages. It isn't that young writers must only write in single sentences until they master one, then two, then three sentences, and so forth. On the contrary, they must always be engaged in writing grander messages for their readers.

At the same time, however, young writers must become effective at thinking in and writing sentences. In this way, they will best learn the basic elements of language construction and use those elements to write their grander messages.

The sentence is a string of language that captures an idea, a thought, an image. It is a sound, a *sentence sound*, in fact. Good writers use this sound to monitor their sentences as they write. Good writers hear the language they write, even as they write it, as ideas and images play out in their minds and on to the paper. To have the sound of the sentence as automatic feedback is a critical part of being able to write well.

One Sentence at a Time brings young writers into both oral and written contact with the constructive properties of sentences. To perform this activity, they will:

- Think of an idea or an image
- Think of a way to bring their idea or image before an audience as a single sentence
- "Read aloud" the sentence they have "written" in their minds
- Write on paper the sentence they have written in their minds
- Read their sentence aloud for audience feedback

 ## Objective

Young writers will mentally construct a sentence and "read" aloud their mental construction. Afterwards, they will write this mental construction on paper and read aloud what they have written.

Conducting the Lesson

1. **Give students a cue for writing.** The cue might be based on a theme. For example, direct students to think of a cloud. Then direct them to think of something they could say about a cloud. Finally, direct them to think of a sentence that contains the word *cloud*, and to include something they might say about a cloud. (Remember they are only working mentally at the moment.)

> **Tip**
>
> To the inevitable question, "How do you spell—?," the teacher's response must be, "Spell it as well as you can."
>
> This doesn't mean spelling isn't important. It just means this is not a spelling lesson and the focus is on the *sentence*.

2. **Listen to six or eight students volunteer their mental sentences.** Occasionally ask, "What is your sentence about?" This focuses attention on the fact that sentences are about ideas and images.

3. **Decide whether to model or to promote on-the-spot revision:** *Modeling* is for the child who needs more time and confidence. *Revision* is for the child who can and will think and respond on the spot.

    Examples: To model, repeat the child's sentence: **It is a puffy cloud**. To focus on revision, ask, "What about the puffy cloud—the puffy cloud what? What else can you say to make the sentence clearer?"

    Children will quickly work their way toward the sound of a sentence, responding, for example, with, "**I like the puffy cloud**." Use this opportunity to give direct feedback to the child by saying, "Now, that's a sentence!"

> **Cue**
>
> Think of a cloud.
>
> Think of something you could write about your cloud.
>
> Write a sentence that includes your cloud and something about it.

©ECS Learning Systems, Inc., San Antonio, TX

4. **After listening to several oral readings of mental sentences, direct the children to write their sentence on paper.** In the second and third grades, one minute is sufficient time for this writing. Most children who are not able to finish their sentence in one minute will eventually be able to finish in the time allotted. As you roam around the room, call on children nearby so you can see what they are reading. Students often revise their writing as they read aloud. Reinforce these oral revisions, then tell them to make their revisions, or to "fix their sentences in writing."

5. **Listen to several children read their revised sentences.** Encourage writers to revise their sentence as they listen to their peers'. Direct young writers to turn in their papers or file them in their portfolios. Remind them that they will be writing sentences every day.

6. **Debrief.** Encourage young writers to remember what they learned about thinking in and writing sentences. Also, suggest that what they wrote this time might be an idea for future writing in their portfolios.

Daily Writing Activities

1. Think of a **paintbrush**. Think of something you can tell about a paintbrush. Think of a sentence that contains the word *paintbrush*, and tell something about a paintbrush.

2. Think of something that is **round**. Write its name on your paper. Write something you can tell about the round thing. Write a sentence about the round thing.

3. Write the name of something that is **red**. Write a sentence about something red. Write another sentence that contains the name of two red things.

4. Write the name of something **cold**. Write the names of two cold things. Write a sentence about one of the cold things. Write a sentence about the other cold thing. Write a sentence that contains the names of two cold things.

5. Think of a **plant**. Make a list of three things you can say about that plant. Write a sentence that contains all three of the things you can say about your plant (green, tall, leaves). Write another sentence in which the three things appear in a different order (tall, leaves, green).

6. On your paper, write the name of something that is **warm**. Write two things you can say about the warm thing. Write a sentence about warm things.

7. Write the name of something that **buckles**. Think of three things you can say about the thing that buckles. Write a sentence that contains the name of the thing that buckles. Write another sentence that contains two of the things you can say about the thing that buckles. Write a sentence about a pet dog that has a pretty collar.

8. Think of a **salt shaker**. Write at least two things you can say about a salt shaker. Write a sentence that contains the two things you can say about a salt shaker.

9. Think of something that will **absorb water**. Think of three things you can say about the thing that absorbs water. Write a sentence that contains the name of the thing that absorbs water and one of the things you can say about it.

> Teachers can apply these activities in their own creative ways and in a variety of subject areas. For example, there are implied applications to science in Activities 5 and 9.

10. Think of a **pencil sharpener**. Make a list of three things you can say about a pencil sharpener. Write a sentence that contains two of the three things you can say about a pencil sharpener.

©ECS Learning Systems, Inc., San Antonio, TX

11. Think of a **piece of paper** you use for writing. List four things you can say about the paper. Write a sentence that contains two of the four things you can say about the paper. Write a sentence that contains the ideas of paper and recycling.

12. Write the name of something that tells **time**. Think of three things you can say about the thing that tells time. Write a sentence that contains the name of the thing that tells time and two things you can say about it.

13. Think of a **place** you would like to be. Write a sentence about the place. List at least four things you can say about the place you would like to be. Write a sentence that contains at least two of the things you can say about this place.

14. Write the name of something you wear on your **head**. List three things you can say about what you have named. Write a sentence that contains two of the three things.

15. Think of something with **holes** in it. List four things you can say about the thing with holes in it. Write a sentence that contains the name of the thing with holes and at least two of the items you listed.

16. Write the name of something that can be used as a **tool**. Write a sentence that tells what this thing can be used for. List three things you can say about this tool. Write a sentence that contains the name of the thing that can be used as a tool and at least two things you can say about it.

17. Think of something you think is **pretty**. Write the name of this thing. List at least five things you can say about what you think is pretty. Write a sentence that contains the name of what you think is pretty and two things you can say about it. Write a sentence that tells why you think it is pretty.

18. Write the name of a **game** you like to play. Write at least five things you can say about the game. Write a sentence that contains the name of the game and one thing you can say about it. Write a sentence that tells why you like to play this game.

19. Write the name of something that **roars**. List four things you can say about this thing that roars. Write a sentence that contains three of the four things.

20. Think of a word that rhymes with *pace*. Write the rhyming word. Think of three things you can say about the rhyming word. Write a sentence using one of the three things.

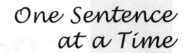
Across the Curriculum

One Sentence at a Time can easily be used in various content areas. The following is an activity based on a science unit on carnivorous and omnivorous animals:

Example: "Class, let's think of an animal that doesn't eat meat." (Cow.) "Write *cow* on your paper. We are going to write a short report about your animal. First, think of one thing you could write about it." (They eat hay.) "Now write a sentence that names your animal and includes the one thing you want to say about it." (*A cow eats hay*.)

"What does your animal do? Think about something your animal does, and write a sentence about that." (*Cows chew a lot and lay around.*)

"Do you think your animal is very important?" (Yes.) "Write a sentence that tells why you think your animal is important." (*Cows are important because they give us milk*.)

This application can occur weekly as the teacher or the children suggest topics for short reports of several sentences. The focus, of course, is the quality of sentences, but the topic is science.

English Language Learners

The following sample dialogue for using **One Sentence at a Time** takes place in an average-sized third-grade class, with 12 Spanish-speaking students who understand directions spoken in English. However, they are only able to write in Spanish, and the teacher speaks no Spanish at all.

Example: "Think of a word for a kind of weather. If I were thinking of a word like that, I might think of *rain*." [Draw a "rain" picture on the board. Stick figures will do.] "Now think of a weather word." (Is *windy* okay?) "Of course. Now everyone, think of a sentence with your word in it."

The children share their sentences orally, then write them on paper. When a student reads a sentence in Spanish, the teacher can ask for a translation from the student or a classmate. A conversation about how the sentence paints a picture should follow, and the lesson can continue with capable bilingual children translating as necessary.

In this sample application, there is writing across two languages, writing in the language for which each student is more comfortable, and public reading and feedback which places neither positive nor negative value on either language performance.

One Sentence at a Time

1. Write the name of a good book you have read.

   _____

2. Write two things you noticed about the book you read.

   _____

   _____

3. Write a sentence that contains one of the things you noticed about the book.

   _____

   _____

4. Write a sentence that tells what the book reminded you of.

   _____

   _____

5. Write a sentence that tells why you think other children might like the book.

   _____

   _____

©ECS Learning Systems, Inc., San Antonio, TX

One Sentence at a Time

1. Write the name of something that floats.

   _____

2. Write three things you can say about the thing that floats.

   a. _____

   b. _____

   c. _____

3. Write a sentence that names the thing that floats and includes item **1** in your list, above.

   _____

   _____

4. Write a sentence that contains items **2** and **3** from your list above.

   _____

   _____

5. Write a sentence about a boat floating on a lake.

   _____

   _____

Get Writing!! Book 1 Grades 2-3   ©ECS Learning Systems, Inc., San Antonio, TX   17

2 Using Ideas to Make Sentences

—The term "main idea" is traditionally associated with paragraphs, but every sentence has a main idea, as well.

▶ Information for the Teacher

Using the sentence to display and expand on a main idea is a basic principle in writing. In the following sentence, there is a main or central idea—a picture, an image:

> **It was a rainy Thursday afternoon when the limo door opened in front of our best downtown hotel, and the woman wearing a long blue dress and diamond necklace emerged and strode through the huge double doors and into our lives.**

The main idea is a woman we do not yet know. There are other ideas in this sentence, but they are all secondary details that modify or qualify the main idea. The implied wealth modifies the woman, as do the limo and the jewels. The woman, however, is the main idea, and the details only support the main idea.

In another sentence about something that locks (a safe deposit box) and three brainstormed ideas (bank, keys, valuables), a sentence in which *vault* is the main idea might be written as follows:

> **The bank's vault had two-hundred safe deposit boxes and three rooms where they kept valuables.**

A sentence in which *valuables* represents the main idea might be written in this way:

> **Our family's valuables were very important to us, so we got a safe deposit box at the bank.**

▶ Objective

Using Ideas to Make Sentences is about thinking in main ideas at the sentence level. Young writers brainstorm ideas in response to a cue. They arrange their own ideas into a sentence and notice how this arrangement influences the main idea.

Tip Young writers will learn that the way they write sentences controls the main idea.

©ECS Learning Systems, Inc., San Antonio, TX

Conducting the Lesson

1. **Pose an idea for brainstorming.** As the students' hands go up, write their ideas on the board.

   Example: "Think of something you can wear on your head." [Hat, helmet, feathers, ribbon, wig.] "Let's pick one and think of something to write. I'm going to pick hat. Think of three things you could write about a hat." [Baseball, football, pretty, colors, and rain.]

2. **As students generate ideas, write them on the board and arrange the ideas into a sentence.**

   Example: (The boy has a hat.) "What is the main idea of this sentence?" (The boy and the hat.)

3. **Listen to two or three student sentences, then ask them to add an idea.**

   Example: "Think of a sentence that has a hat in it plus one of the color words." **(I see a green hat on the boy.)** "Now, what is the main idea of the sentence?" (The green hat and the boy.)

4. **Ask the children to write their own sentences using** *hat* **and any two other ideas from the list on the board.** Show them how this influences the main idea of the sentence.

   Example: [The man in the blue baseball hat got a hit.] "What do you see?" (I see a baseball player running to the base after hitting the ball.) "This sentence makes a picture for us. The player running to first base after getting a hit is the main idea of the sentence."

5. **Listen to several readings and solicit comments about the main idea from listeners.** Young writers must see that their writing generates ideas in listeners (readers).

Provide sufficient time for writing, usually around one minute. When the hands go up for spelling help, the best response, is, "Spell the word as well as you can. You will have a chance to spell it better later." If some children are clearly unable to write further without help, write accurate spellings at the top of their papers.

6. **Follow up with an independent writing assignment (e.g., p. 14, Number 13 or 14).** Offer an extra Ticket to Recess later in the day for those who complete the assignment, and give a homework assignment to those who do not.

7. **Remind students that the writing they submit to the teacher or to a peer should be as accurate or correct as they can make it. Explain:** "When the paper is on your side of the desk, it is your business; when it leaves your desk, it has to be done right."

> Children may ask their neighbor or the teacher for help, or look up words on a "Word Wall" or in their own "Word Book."

©ECS Learning Systems, Inc., San Antonio, TX

 Daily Writing Activities

1. Think of something that has **holes**. Write its name. List five things you could write about the thing that has holes. Write a sentence that names the thing that has holes and includes two of the things you could write about it. Write the main idea of your sentence.

2. Think of something that needs **electricity** to work. Write its name on your paper. List three things you could write about the thing that needs electricity to work. Write a sentence that names the item and includes one of the ideas on your list. Ask someone to read your sentence and tell you what the main idea is.

3. Write the name of something that will **float in air**. List three things you could write about it. Add two more items to your list. Write a sentence about something that floats in air. Write the main idea of your sentence. Ask someone to read your sentence and tell you the main idea. Write what someone else thinks is the main idea of your sentence.

4. Write the name of something that will **absorb water**. List two things you could write about it. List two more things you could write about it. Write a sentence that names the thing that absorbs water and includes two of the things you could say about it. Write the main idea of your sentence.

5. Think of a **pencil sharpener**. Write a sentence that includes the words "pencil sharpener." Think of what a pencil sharpener looks like. Write a sentence that tells what a pencil sharpener looks like. Write the main idea of your sentence. Think about how a person sharpens a pencil. Write a sentence that tells how a pencil sharpener works. Ask someone to read your sentence and tell you the main idea.

6. Write the name of something you use to **measure time**. List three things you could say about it. Write a sentence about something that measures time, and be sure the main idea is about the item you named.

7. Think of a **place** where you would like to be. Write its name on your paper. List three things you could write about this place. Write a sentence about this place, and include two of the items from your list in your sentence. Write the main idea of your sentence.

8. Write the name of a **tool** that you might find in a **garage**. Write what the tool is used for. Write a sentence about a tool that you might find in a garage, and include what it might be used for. Write the main idea of your sentence and ask someone else if he or she agrees with what you think is your main idea.

Get Writing!! Book 1 Grades 2-3   ©ECS Learning Systems, Inc., San Antonio, TX   21

9. Think about a **refrigerator**. Write the name of something you might find in a refrigerator. Write a sentence about something you might find in a refrigerator. Read your sentence and think of what the main idea is. Write another sentence about a refrigerator in which the main idea is left-overs.

10. Think of a **refrigerator** again. This time think of what a refrigerator looks like. Write a sentence in which the main idea is what a refrigerator looks like. Ask someone to read your sentence and tell you if the main idea is about what a refrigerator looks like.

11. Write the name of something you do that makes you **perspire**. Think of three things you could write about something that makes you perspire and write them on a list. Write a sentence about something you do that makes you perspire. What is the main idea in your sentence? Find a reader who agrees with you about the main idea.

12. Think of a **game** you would like to write about. Write its name. Write a sentence that includes the name of the game and something about why you like the game. Think of two things you could tell someone about the game. Write a sentence in which the main idea is how much fun the game is to play.

13. Think of something you have at **home** that you would like to have at **school**. Write its name on your paper. Think about why you would like to have the item at school. Think of two things you could write about the item. Write a sentence about the item you have at home and would like to have at school. What is the main idea of your sentence? Check with a person sitting near you to see if he or she agrees with what you think the main idea is.

14. Think of **clouds**. List at least three things you could write about clouds. Write a sentence about clouds and include at least two of the items from your list. Put a picture of a cloud in your mind. Write a sentence in which the main idea is the picture you have in your head.

15. Write the name of something that **roars**. List four things you could write about it. Write a sentence in which the main idea is about an animal that roars.

 ## Across the Curriculum

This is the perfect opportunity to help young writers acquire **control** over words. For example, pose the following continuum on the board, and then ask students to add to the list:

Things That Float	**Things That Do Not Float**
Rubber Ball	*Rocks*

List items as they are called out by the students. Pose the possibility that other items might go on a third list between "Things That Float" and "Things That Do Not Float."

As children think actively in words, they gain control over them. New words can carry meaning for them because they know many of the words that relate in some way to the target word. They know the word *hot* because they know *cold* and *frosty*, *steaming*, *humid*, and *warm*, and so forth. They know *absorb* because they know many things that are absorbent (*cloth*, *celery*, and *newspaper*). Children can also gain greater control over specialized words by working with synonyms, antonyms, descriptions, and so forth.

 ## English Language Learners

In **Using Ideas to Make Sentences** young writers get feedback from peers about the main ideas in their sentences. Since main ideas occur in all languages, pairs of children can talk and write about main ideas in any language.

The ability to speak English in an informal setting does not necessarily indicate language competence with academic content. However, as children talk to one another in their native langue about subjects of academic content, their conversation bridges the gap between playground and academic language. This should be instructive for the teacher. Any classroom learning activity that causes children to talk with one another, especially about academic content, is enormously important.

Get Writing!! Book 1 Grades 2-3   ©ECS Learning Systems, Inc., San Antonio, TX   23

Language Activity Sheet
Using Ideas to Make Sentences

1. Think of something that makes a **pleasant sound**. Write its name.

   _____

2. List at least three things you could write about the thing that makes a pleasant sound.

   a. _____

   b. _____

   c. _____

3. Write a sentence that includes one of the items on your list.

   _____

   _____

4. Write a sentence that names something that makes a pleasant sound. Include two items from your list.

   _____

   _____

Language Activity Sheet
Using Ideas to Make Sentences

1. Write the name of something that is **cold**.

    _____

2. List at least five things you could write about the cold thing you named above.

    a. _____

    b. _____

    c. _____

    d. _____

    e. _____

3. Write a sentence about something that is cold, and use at least two items from your list.

    _____

    _____

4. Write another sentence, and this time name the cold thing and use three items from your list.

    _____

    _____

©ECS Learning Systems, Inc., San Antonio, TX

3 Main Ideas in Double Sentence Strings

—Main ideas in sentences are enlarged by the details in supporting sentences.

 ## Information for the Teacher

Writing in double sentence strings helps young writers understand the role of sentences in the development of main ideas. This activity is about writing two related sentences with specific attention to the main idea. As young writers become fluent in writing one sentence at a time and recognizing main ideas, they should immediately begin deliberate and systematic practice with **Main Ideas in Double Sentence Strings**.

In **Main Ideas in Double Sentence Strings**, young writers:

- Share orally the sentences they write in their minds

- Put sentences on paper to be read aloud

- Specify the main idea developed in their double sentence string

In addition, teachers will:

- Call attention to devices that promote cohesion between sentences

- Reflect on student readings

- Encourage class feedback about the main ideas in student readings

- Encourage revisions of student writing to support main idea

 ## Objective

Young writers will mentally construct, verbalize, write on paper, then read aloud for feedback, their double sentence strings in response to teacher cue.

 Every piece of writing read aloud is a sound from which children learn. It is important when introducing a new concept, therefore, to call first on young writers who are likely to have the right answers. The greatest teaching and learning merit is in using accurate models as instructional devices.

©ECS Learning Systems, Inc., San Antonio, TX

Conducting the Lesson

1. **Ask students to recall writing in single sentences and writing about main ideas.** Let them know that they will now be writing about their ideas in two sentences.

   Example: "Think back to your writing when you were putting ideas into single sentences. You thought of an idea and things to say about it, then you wrote a sentence using your idea. We're going to do that again, but this time you get to write two sentences!"

   Tip While some second-and third-graders will not understand these directions the first time, more explanation and modeling merely makes everyone follow the teacher's lead. The best option is to say, "If you don't understand exactly what we're going to do here, wait and watch carefully what we do next. Then it will make more sense."

2. **Give students a cue for writing, and write their ideas on the board.**

   Example: "Think of something that is very small." (A ladybug.) (A newborn kitten.) (A mouse.) "Let's start with a ladybug. What can we say about it?" (It's red.) (It flies.) (It eats some bad stuff off the leaves.)

3. **Ask students to mentally construct two sentences that include three of the ideas on the board.** They may put two ideas into one sentence and one into the other, or may put all three ideas into one sentence and use the other sentence to explain. But they must have two sentences in a row and use three of the ideas on the board.

4. **Carefully select the best student model of double sentences and share it with the class.** Before sharing this model with the class, listen as you walk around the room to two or three whispered tries at double sentences. Be certain to respond to each try with positive feedback.

   Cue Think of a main idea. Think of a way to arrange your ideas about the main idea into a double sentence string.

Get Writing!! Book 1 Grades 2-3   ©ECS Learning Systems, Inc., San Antonio, TX   27

Main Ideas in Double Sentence Strings

5. **As a volunteer student reads the model double sentence string, ask the class to identify the two separate sentences.**

After this first instance of directing a volunteer step by step, a model will be established for other students to follow.

Example: "Read your double sentence string." (**The little ladybug had red on her back. She flew to a new branch**.) "How many sentences did you hear?" (Two.)

6. **Demonstrate to the class the cohesiveness between two sentences in the model double sentence strings.** Explain to the class that the gluing together of sentences is called *cohesion*. Advise students that they will need to know this word in the eighth grade, but for now this will be called "making sentences go together."

Example: "Someone read just their second sentence for us." (**She flew to a new branch**.) "Who is the '*She*' in the second sentence?" (The ladybug!) "Yes, but how did you know?" (It's in the first sentence!) "Yes! When you talk about the ladybug in the first sentence and then use '*She*' to start the second sentence, you are gluing the two sentences together."

7. **Ask students to identify the main idea of each sentence in a model double sentence string.**

Example: "What is the main idea of this double sentence string: **The little ladybug had red on her back. She flew to a new branch**." (It is a ladybug and she had to go to a new branch for something to eat.) "Well, what about the first sentence? What is the main idea of that one?" (A red lady bug.)

"How about the main idea of the second sentence? What do you think it is?" (The ladybug went to a new branch.)

8. **Point out the way sentences go together to make the whole main idea.**

Example: "The second sentence just says it's '*she*.' How do we know the '*she*' is a ladybug?" (It's in the first sentence.) "So that means the two sentences have to be together to make the whole main idea?" (Yeah.)

9. **If time allows, ask for new volunteers and repeat Numbers 1-8.**

Tip

It nearly always happens that one of the following two scenarios occurs during the first couple of double sentence string writing sessions:

Scenario 1: A young writer will read (either from a mental construction or from the paper) a sentence that accommodates all three ideas:

Example: (The tiny ladybug was eating and she had to fly away because there was a bird that wanted to eat her.) "Now that's a sentence filled with ideas! Read it again, and listen as you read. I want you to count the sentences you hear. And everyone else, listen to the sounds so you can count the sentences." **(The tiny ladybug was eating and she had to fly away because there was a bird that wanted to eat her.)** "How many sentences did you read?" (Two.)

By reading the student's sentence directly from the paper, you will see that the student has orally broken the sentence at *eating* and started the new sentence with *and*. Revise the sentence(s) right over the student's shoulder:

"If you want to write it the way you have it on your paper, you put a comma between *eating* and *and*. That will give you one sentence. But if you want two sentences, put a period after eating, scratch out the *and*, and begin the new sentence with a capital letter. Now, read it the way we revised it." **(The tiny ladybug was eating. She had to fly away because there was a bird that wanted to eat her.)** "Terrific! What is the main idea of your double sentence string?"

[Continue the conversation as with Number 7, above.]

Scenario 2: A young writer will read one or two non-sentences:

Example: (Red ladybug. It flies away.) "You have a terrific idea working there. Let's see. What if we make a sentence that will read: **A red ladybug is flying away.** What might be your second sentence?" **(She has to get away from the bird.)** "Good for you. Look up on the board as I write your double sentence string. Then write it on your paper."

When the sentences are on the board, the teacher will direct the student to read them aloud and then to write them on paper.

10. **Work with student volunteers to see that they do it *RIGHT*.** During the first two or three double sentence writing sessions, there may be some need to work carefully through scenarios similar to those in Number 7, above. However, once the pattern is set and the children have learned the pattern, there will be little or no need for direct instruction.

Main Ideas in Double Sentence Strings

 ## Daily Writing Activities

1. Think of something that you sometimes eat for dinner. Think of three things you could write about it. Think of a way to write one sentence that contains something you eat for dinner plus one of the things you could write about it. Now think of a way that you could write a double sentence string that includes something you eat for dinner and two things you could write about it. Decide the main idea of your double sentence string. Read your double sentence string to someone and ask what (s)he thinks is the main idea.

2. Think of an animal that might make a good pet. In your head, write a sentence in which the pet is the main idea. List three things you could write about the pet. Write a double sentence string that includes two of the three things you could say about the pet. After you have written the double sentence string, write its main idea in no more than five words.

3. List words about the weather. Choose one weather word as the main idea for a sentence. Write a sentence in which something about the weather is the main idea. Write a double sentence string in which something about the weather is the main idea. Share your double sentence string with someone and ask if (s)he thinks the main idea is the same as the one you tried to write.

4. Think of three things you could write about one of your friends. Select one of the three and write a double sentence string in which the main idea is the best thing about your friend. Share your writing with your friend.

5. Think of something you know how to do. Write one sentence that tells about what you know how to do. Write a double sentence string in which the main idea is something you know how to do.

6. Write the name of a book you have read. Think about the book, and write what you noticed when you read it. Write a double sentence string in which the main idea is what you noticed when you read the book.

7. Think about what you enjoy watching on television. Think of two reasons why you enjoy watching a certain television program. Write a double sentence string in which the main idea is why you enjoy a certain television program.

8. Think about the kitchen in your house. Write three things that come to your mind when you think about your kitchen. Write a double sentence string in which the main idea is something about the kitchen where you live.

©ECS Learning Systems, Inc., San Antonio, TX

 ## Across the Curriculum

Main Ideas in Double Sentences is a fine opportunity to begin helping young writers to understand the principle of "constructing" ideas in short pieces of writing.

Examples:

1. Write a double sentence string in which the main idea is what subtraction means.

2. Write a double sentence string in which the main idea is how to subtract 26 from 40.

There are two values in such writing. First, it gives young writers the opportunity to use writing as a learning device. As they have to think of ways to make subtraction into a main idea in two sentences, they must think about subtraction in a very deliberate manner. The writing provides a way for youngsters to think through ideas and concepts and to clarify their thinking. Second, as the teacher collects children's double sentence strings about subtraction, understandings in that content area can be assessed.

 ## English Language Learners

The principle of main idea is not specific to any one language. Therefore, **Main Ideas in Double Sentence Strings** can be used in any language. To encourage English, however, it is necessary that there be at least one person in the classroom who can not only understand the target language, but also translate into English.

When a young writer reads in a language the teacher doesn't understand, (s)he can listen and call on another child to translate it. When the sentence is translated, the young writer can then be asked to reread the sentence in the original language and to say what the main idea is. The young writer whose English proficiency allows for basic interpersonal communication can then give the main idea of his/her sentence. An entire 20-minute lesson can be conducted that way.

Main Ideas in Double Sentence Strings

1. Think of something you think is **very heavy**. Write its name.

   _____

2. Write a sentence in which the main idea is something that is very heavy.

   _____

   _____

3. List three things you could write about the heavy object you named above.

   a. _____

   b. _____

   c. _____

4. Write a double sentence string that names the heavy object and includes at least one of the things you could say about the heavy object.

   _____

   _____

   _____

5. In one sentence, write the main idea of your double sentence string.

   _____

   _____

Get Writing!! Book 1 Grades 2-3   ©ECS Learning Systems, Inc., San Antonio, TX

Language Activity Sheet
Main Ideas in Double Sentence Strings

1. Write the name of an animal you might find in a **zoo**.

   _____

2. Write a sentence in which the main idea is something about the animal you named above.

   _____

   _____

3. Write a word that tells the color of the animal.

   _____

4. Write a word that tells the size of the animal.

   _____

5. Write a word that tells what the animal eats.

   _____

6. Write a double sentence string that includes something about at least two of the ideas you wrote above.

   _____

   _____

   _____

4 Planning Words in Sentences

—Writing is not hopeful. Writing is purposeful.

Information for the Teacher

When some people—especially young writers—write, they hope it will work. They start with a capital letter and hope something happens before they get to the period. Part of learning to write well is *automatic planning*. This does not mean outlining an essay or deciding the plot-line in a story, or even brainstorming and clustering for prewriting. It means thinking about the language as it is being written.

Arriving at this level of skill and confidence demands practice, and some practice must focus on the purposefulness of writing. Such practice may not look like real writing, but is part of the learning. This practice best occurs on a periodic basis, perhaps as a series of early lessons during which students gain control over the activity, then as "quickwrites" that consume only a few moments several times per month.

Planning Words in Sentences is about practicing purposefulness in early writing. It is absolutely not all there is in learning to write, and it is absolutely not the *anchor* of learning to write. It is only part of a comprehensive writing program. To perform this activity students will:

- Plan and mentally write a sentence in which two, three, then four of the words begin with the same letter
- Orally share their sentences
- Write their sentences on paper
- Craft single sentences on the basis of letter cues that cause them to consider every word deliberately.

Objective

Young writers will craft single sentences on the basis of letter cues that cause them to consider every word deliberately.

 ## Conducting the Lesson

1. **On the board, write a sentence in which two of the words begin with a specified letter.**

   Example: "I would like you to think of a special sentence today. Think of a way to write a sentence in which two of the words begin with **W**. If I were going to make a sentence like that, I might write it this way: [Write on the board] **Willy went to the store**. Now you think of a sentence that has two words that begin with **W**."

2. **Encourage the students to "write their sentences in their heads and push them out of their mouths."** Doing this eliminates two enormous problems in the writing program for primary children. One, they don't have to spell anything. And, two, without the laborious process of drawing their letters, they can "write" in seconds.

 Resist the urge to encourage greater variety or to ask students to remember last week's spelling words, even though they seem to use the same words in their sentences.

3. **After listening to several sentences, change the cue to three words that begin with the selected letter.**

 It is easy to promote what we want from young writers merely by changing the cue. The simple addition of another word or two will immediately produce variety in sentences.

Children delight in the compelling cognitive activities of manipulating language and problem-solving. They are very deliberate about this kind of writing, and think carefully about nearly every word—the very purpose of the activity.

4. **Repeat 1-3.** As soon as children understand the writing task with several words that begin with **W**, they will have a good grasp on how this activity works. Everything that follows in the lesson is merely a variation on the same theme.

 Think of a sentence in which two, three, then four of the words begin with the letter **W**.

Get Writing!! Book 1 Grades 2-3   ©ECS Learning Systems, Inc., San Antonio, TX   35

5. **After they have mentally generated several sentences containing four words that begin with the same letter, direct students to write one of their sentences on paper.**

   Example: "Now, I want you to write a sentence like that on paper. I want you to write a sentence in which four words begin with **W**. If you do not know how to spell some words, remember the "three before me" rule. Always ask three people or look in three places before you ask me how to spell a word. I want you to hand me your **W**-word sentences as your ticket to recess."

6. **Make it routine to ask students to share their writings (single sentences, double sentences, etc.) aloud.** Don't forget the power of bringing oral language into the writing program. The sound of well-constructed language is invaluable and children love the sharing.

With each writing session, everyone should put something on paper from the writing in their heads. By using formal oral language in the writing program, we not only promote a whole conception of language behavior, we also help the children become increasingly fluent.

 ## Daily Writing Activities

1. Write a sentence in which at least three words begin with **H**. (**Note to Teacher:** This prompt can be repeated with most of the letters of the alphabet. Letters like **X** and **Z** are probably too difficult for primary children to use in this activity. Also, consonants work better than vowels, and vowels like **I** and **A** work better than the others.)

2. Write a sentence in which two words end with the letter **r**. (**Note to Teacher:** This prompt can be repeated with several high-frequency letters. **G**, **M**, **N**, for instance, are good letters for this prompt, but **H** tends not to work very well when children are particularly young. Try various letters and see what happens.)

3. Write a sentence that contains five **Rs**. (**Note to Teacher:** In this prompt, the words don't have to begin with **R**. The rule is that the sentence must just have five of them in it. **Example: Rules are rough to follow for boys named Ralph.**)

4. Write a sentence that contains eleven vowels.

5. Write a sentence in which there are nine "hump" letters (**n-m-r-h**).

6. Write a sentence in which no word has more than four letters. **Example: Pat had five nice cats who only ate mice when they were not mad.**

7. Write a sentence of at least six words in which every word has an even number of letters. **Example: We don't have very many pretty pictures in this room.**

8. Write a sentence in which each word begins with the letter **E. Example: Every evening Eric eats eight eggplants.**

9. Write a sentence in which the letter **E** is not used at all. **Example: My watch is too slow.**

10. If your name were David, and you were to write a five-word sentence in which each word began with the letters from your name, the sentence might read: **David and Vivian issued directions.** Write a sentence in which each word begins with a letter from David's name. (**Note to Teacher:** It is best to set this one up on the board so the children can then set up their own in the same manner.)

    Example:

    D _____ a _____ v _____ i _____ d _____

Get Writing!! Book 1 Grades 2-3   ©ECS Learning Systems, Inc., San Antonio, TX   37

Planning Words in Sentences

11. Write a sentence is which each word begins with a letter from your name (see Number 10.). Continue setting up the sentence design on the board until the children begin setting up their own without being told.

C_____ a_____ r_____ l_____ a_____

12. Write a sentence every day in which each word begins with letters from the name of a student in the room. The sentence will be the Ticket to Recess.

13. Write a sentence in which each word begins with a letter from the name of a [favorite athletic hero, President of the United States, local mayor, member of Congress, and so forth].

14. Write a sentence in which each word begins with a letter from one of the social studies words.

I_____ s_____ l_____ a_____ n_____ d_____

15. Write a sentence that contains no more than five vowels.

16. Write a sentence of at least seven words. The only vowel you may use is **e**. You may use words that have other vowels, but you may not write the vowels. See if your friends can read your sentence written that way. **Example**: *pony* becomes **pny**; *beautiful* becomes **betfl**.

17. Write a sentence in which each word begins with a letter from the name of an animal.

E_____ l_____ e_____ p_____ h_____ a_____ n_____ t_____

> *Tip*
>
> Automatic writing comes with practice, and perfect practice makes perfect. There are about 30 people in the room, that's 30 sentences that force deliberate attention to sentence construction.

©ECS Learning Systems, Inc., San Antonio, TX

Across the Curriculum

This activity can be used to focus attention on vocabulary in the content areas. It can also be used as an ancillary spelling activity. The initial letter of each word is the focus letter. Planning and writing are focused on the sentence.

English Language Learners

Planning Words in Sentences offers students working in a new language the opportunity to think deliberately about how the new language works. Language is learned through *use*, and the use itself must have merit and payoff. In this activity, the merit is solving a puzzle, the payoff is the solution which is, of course, a sentence.

Early on, it is best to work these sentence puzzles in a large group. The whole class conversation brings everyone to grips with the nature of the puzzle and encourages everyone to suggest ideas and participate in judgements of feasibility. In this sample application, there is writing across two languages, writing in the language for which each student is more comfortable, and public reading and feedback which places neither positive nor negative value on either language performance.

> This activity should not lead the language program in a class where the majority of children do not speak English as a native language, but rather be an integral part of such a program.

Get Writing!! Book 1 Grades 2-3   ©ECS Learning Systems, Inc., San Antonio, TX   39

Language Activity Sheet
Planning Words in Sentences

1. There are many kinds of birds. One we can see in the spring is the robin. That is a five-letter word: **r-o-b-i-n**. If you wrote a sentence in which the first word began with **R**, it might begin like this.

Running   o _____   b _____   i _____   n _____

What might be the second word that begins with **O**? The third word begins with **B**. The fourth word begins with **I**. The fifth word begins with **N**.

Example:

Running on beaches is nice.

2. Now it is your turn to write a sentence with **robin**.

R _____   o _____   b _____   i _____   n _____

3. Now do it again with **crow**.

C _____   r _____   o _____   w _____

©ECS Learning Systems, Inc., San Antonio, TX

Language Activity Sheet
Planning Words in Sentences

1. Think of your favorite male person on television. Write the letters of his name at the beginning of the blanks below. You can add more blanks if you need to.

   _____   _____   _____   _____

   _____   _____   _____   _____

2. Write a sentence in which each word begins with the first letter of your favorite male television person's name.

   _____

   _____

3. Write a sentence in which each word begins with the letters in the name of your favorite female person on television.

   _____   _____   _____   _____

   _____   _____   _____   _____

4. Write a sentence for one of the words below.

   F _____   e _____   m_____   a _____

   l _____   e _____

   M _____   a _____   l _____   e _____

5 Writing Sentences with Capital Letters and End Marks

—When writers talk about good writing, they mean writing that works, not with the effort of "figuring it out," but on a clear first read.

 ## Information for the Teacher

Children sometimes get the message that if readers can figure out what their printing means, they don't have to be too concerned about mechanical precision. Unfortunately, "figuring it out" is not effective communication.

Capital Letters and End Marks in Sentences is the first of many lessons in this writing program committed to mastery of mechanical control. As soon as young writers are writing sentences, they need to pay attention to the mechanical conventions that make sentences work clearly for both writers and readers. The most basic conventions are the two that mark the beginning and end of a sentence.

In writing, these three principles are important—

- Mechanical control is important in learning to write well.

- Skill with mechanical control is progressive, growing with practice and attention to accuracy.

- Only the writer is responsible for the learning, practice, and mechanical precision of his/her written work.

Attention to mechanical control occurs during as well as after writing. As young writers learn to write increasingly well, they handle the mechanical aspects of written language when they plan, draft, and edit. Young writers do not learn to capitalize and punctuate by memorizing conventions or by editing other people's writing on worksheets or on the board. They learn by using proper capitalization and punctuation in their own writing.

 ## Objective

As young writers become more conscious of the writing process, they will focus attention on beginning their sentences with capital letters and using appropriate end marks.

Get Writing!! Book 1 Grades 2-3   ©ECS Learning Systems, Inc., San Antonio, TX

Conducting the Lesson

1. **Give students a sentence cue.** When most of the children have a sentence written in their heads, give them one minute to write it on paper. A one-minute time frame eliminates most of the inevitable procrastination that occurs when children write.

> **Tip**
>
> There is nothing sacred about adhering to 60 seconds, but most children can keep up with a relatively rapid pace in the classroom. Timing doesn't interfere with creativity. In fact, most creativity is accomplished against deadlines.

2. **Call on volunteers and read over their shoulders as they read aloud.**

3. **Make reinforcing comments in response to the reading.** When a student reads from a sentence that lacks a capital letter and/or end mark, lean over and whisper your corrections in the child's ear.

4. **Talk to students about their accountability for mechanical precision in their own writing.** As the teacher demands adherence to the convention and as students focus on it, the probability increases that capital letters and end marks will be used correctly.

   Example: "When did you first find out about capital letters at the beginning of sentences?" (In kindergarten.) "That's right. From now on I want to see every sentence begin with a capital letter. Think about capital letters at the beginning of sentences. I will notice every time you write a sentence without one, and you will need to fix the error. Does everyone understand?"

5. **Repeat Numbers 1-3, focusing on periods at the end of sentences.**

> **Cue**
>
> Think of a sentence that includes something about an old man.
>
> Write on paper your sentence about an old man down.
>
> Be sure to use a capital letter at the beginning and a mark to show that the sentence is finished.

6. **Repeat Numbers 1-3, asking for sentences requiring question marks.**

7. **Repeat Numbers 1-3, asking for sentences requiring exclamation marks.** It is very difficult to get students to come up with a sentence that requires an exclamation mark without asking for one directly. Give students an example, then ask them to write a sentence that requires an exclamation mark at the end.

   Example: I love my new puppy!

8. **Debrief.** Make students conscious of distinctions between end marks. Even though this is not new information for second-and third-grade students, it is important to review the distinctions between end marks.

Tip: If second- and third-grade teachers focus students' attention on these activities every day, fourth-grade teachers will have students who rarely make capitalization and end mark errors.

 ## Daily Writing Activities

Any writing activity that causes young writers to compose single sentences satisfies basic writing activities for **Capital Letters and End Marks in Sentences**.

These daily activities can be posted as an independent writing each morning with the children's writing used as their ticket to recess. The writing takes 30 seconds, and in the process, everyone practices two critical conventions every day.

1. Write a sentence that contains your name.

2. Write a sentence that begins with your name.

3. Write a sentence that contains the name of your teacher.

4. Write a sentence in which the main idea is something you like to eat.

5. Write a sentence that tells about a book you read in school.

6. Write a sentence that tells about something you read at home.

7. Write a sentence in which the main idea is something about where you live.

8. Write a sentence that contains the word *shirt*.

9. Write a sentence that contains the word *hawk*.

10. Write a sentence that contains a new word from social studies.

Get Writing!! Book 1 Grades 2-3   ©ECS Learning Systems, Inc., San Antonio, TX   45

Writing Sentences with Capital Letters and End Marks

Each of the writing activities below requires an initial capital letter and an end mark. Such daily writing activities, in which deliberate attention is called to the mechanical conventions, lead young writers toward automatic mechanical control.

The writing activities below all require question marks at the end of sentences. They all require a capital letter to begin the sentences, as well. It is helpful for young writers to practice using the high frequency mechanical conventions *in writing* every day until they are automatic.

11. Write a sentence that ends with a question mark.

12. Write a sentence that contains the name of your friend and ends with a question mark.

13. Write a sentence that asks a question about the weather.

14. Write a sentence that asks a question about a character in a book the whole class is reading.

15. Write a sentence in which you ask your teacher a question.

16. Write a double sentence string in which one of the sentences requires a question mark at the end.

17. Write a double sentence string in which the first sentence requires a question mark and the second sentence requires a period.

18. Find a question sentence in one of your books. Copy the question sentence on your paper. Rewrite the question sentence so that it contains two more words.

19. Write a question sentence that contains a color word.

20. Write a double sentence string in which you ask a writing partner a question. Ask your writing partner to write an answer to your question.

Across the Curriculum

Because practice is the key to using mechanical conventions *automatically* in writing, any situation that promotes attention to initial capital letters and end marks is useful. There is no reason, therefore, why the practice must occur only in language arts or writing periods.

Students often have greater difficulty in content-area reading than in literature narratives because of the vocabulary. The traditional strategy is to find the words in the glossary, write their definitions, and then write sentences that contain them.

In **Capital Letters and End Marks in Sentences**, prompt sentences require more than random placement of target words. Children can begin with a capital letter, then drop in a word after the opening article and finish a sentence (e.g., **The island has trees on it.**). As an alternative, direct students to write a five-word sentence that contains the word *island*. Then ask them to write a five-word sentence in which *island* is in the third, fourth, then fifth position.

Example Sentences: *Island* is a geography word.
Those islands are far away.
Four green islands floated there.
It was an island fantasy.
No man is an island.

English Language Learners

As children progress to increased language proficiency, they develop the ability to use language for academic, rather than mere face-to-face, communication. One of the objectives of second language instruction is to increase academic or cognitive language ability.

Most languages use meaning markers to enhance written communication. In English, we call them capitalization and punctuation. Children who are able to read in their native language are familiar with the concept of meaning markers in the context of this native language.

If presented carefully, the writing requirements in this section can provide the confidence necessary to develop a sense of language competence in children whose native language is not English. With **Capital Letters and End Marks** children think and compose—and do it properly.

Writing Sentences with Capital Letters and End Marks

1. Write a sentence that ends with a period.

   _____

   _____

2. Write a sentence that ends with a question mark.

   _____

   _____

3. Write a sentence that ends with a period by putting one word in each empty blank below.

   _____ _____ rain _____ _____ .

4. Write a sentence that ends with a question mark by putting one word in each empty blank below.

   _____ _____ rain _____ _____ ?

5. Write a sentence in which the main idea is something about a **bicycle**. Use a question mark at the end of your sentence.

   _____

   _____

   _____

Writing Sentences with Capital Letters and End Marks

One way to think about how sentences work is to rewrite one that ends with a period so it must end with a question mark.

Example:

> **The boy and his sister went to the store to buy a bag of peaches.**

> **Did that boy and his sister go to the store to buy a bag of peaches?**

1. Rewrite the following sentence so that it must end with a question mark.

Grandpa ate his dinner and went to sit in his chair. _____

_____

_____

2. Rewrite this sentence so that it must end with a period.

Was that a lion eating his dinner on the rock at the zoo? _____

_____

_____

3. Write a sentence in which the main idea is something you can drink. Make your sentence end with a period.

_____

_____

4. Rewrite your sentence on the other side of this page so it must end with a question mark.

6 Writing Sentences with Rhyming Words

—*Working with rhyming words promotes sentence thinking, writing, and listening.*

 ## Information for the Teacher

Language arts programs in the primary grades are directed in part toward the development of a sensitivity to the sounds of language and the ability to manage these sounds. From a natural linguistic sensitivity, children often generate long lists of rhyming words while playing with language. In **Writing Sentences with Rhyming Words**, young writers have the opportunity to generate words and ideas from rhyming cues and to think of ways to use these words and ideas to create sentences.

In **Writing Sentences with Rhyming Words**, young writers will:

- Produce rhyming words in response to a teacher prompt or cue

- Make lists of their own or offer rhyming words aloud which the teacher will write on the board or transparencies

- Write sentences mentally that include their rhyming words and then write these sentences on paper

- Learn to recognize non-sentences and revise them into better sentences

- Review the use of capital letters and end marks in sentences

 ## Objective

Young writers will produce rhyming words in response to teacher prompts. They will either make lists of their own, or will offer words aloud which the teacher will write on the board or transparencies. They will then write sentences that include their rhyming words.

 ## Conducting the Lesson

1. **Give students a cue for a rhyming word.** For example, direct them to think of the word *rake*. Then direct them to think of a word that rhymes with *rake*. Write their rhyming words on the board.

2. **Ask students to suggest other words that rhyme with *rake* and *make*, and write their suggestions on the board or on transparencies for the overhead projector.** Student suggestions may include such words as *cake, take, bake, fake, lake, sake,* and *wake*. Acknowledge their suggestions and write them on the board.

    If, for example, someone calls out *turtle*, acknowledge the suggestion by writing it on the board as well, but do not list it with the rhyming words. As you write say, "That's a word. *Turtle* is a word."

3. **Ask students to think of a way to write a sentence using one word from the list of rhyming words.** Remind them that writing is something that first goes on in their heads, and then through the pencil to their paper.

4. **Ask volunteers to "read" their mentally-constructed sentences aloud.** Comment regularly on their insights and the quality of their sentences.

    Example: "Oh, your sentence has two of the rhyming words in it. Good for you."

5. **Ask students to think of a sentence that contains another word from the list of rhyming words and write it down on paper.** Remind them to first "write" the sentence in their heads. Then, after several seconds, ask them to write the sentence on paper. Give them one minute to finish. In approximately 45 seconds, give them a signal to finish their sentences.

6. **When most of the students have finished, ask for volunteers to read their sentences aloud from their papers.** Ask students who are not finished to keep writing until they are finished.

7. **Call on writers nearby so you can see that they are actually reading what they wrote.** Most students will actually read their work for the very first time when they share aloud.

Get Writing!! Book 1 Grades 2-3   ©ECS Learning Systems, Inc., San Antonio, TX   51

Writing Sentences with Rhyming Words

8. **As students read, call attention to any revisions that change what is actually written on paper.**

   Example: "Oh, you made a change when you read it aloud. Read it again, and this time read your sentence the way you have it written."

9. **Ask the student to revise the sentence.** "When you listen to your own writing, you can hear some of the revisions you need to make." Then say to the larger group, "That's why I remind you to read your work to yourself. You can hear your own writing that way."

10. **Guide students in revisions of non-sentences.** When a student reads a non-sentence, work with it carefully to ensure it is revised into a sentence before the session is over. After checking to see that the student has indeed written a non-sentence, ask the class for their attention as you explain how to revise it into a sentence.

    Example: [Student reads] (**It the lake in summer**.) "Let's see what we can do here. Class, listen to us work on the sentence. You wrote about the lake in the summer. Tell me something about the lake in the summer." (**It's pretty in the night**.) "Ah, yes, I'll bet it is. Listen to this sentence: **The lake is pretty on a summer night.** Is that what you would like to have in your sentence?"

    As the answer is almost always "Yes," or an affirmative nod, ask the student to listen again to the sound of the revised sentence and to say it back to you. Acknowledge the revision and ask the student to write it on paper.

    Listen to several other student sentences, then ask the first student to read the revised non-sentence. When the student reads the sentence in its revised form, acknowledge the revision again by saying, "Terrific, [student's name]. You revised your writing to make it work. Good for you."

11. **On another day, ask students to prepare for more sentence writing by making a new list of rhyming words. Give them the word _float_ as a cue.** Ask, "Who can tell us a word that rhymes with _float_?" (Students may suggest _boat_, _coat_, _goat_, _moat_, and _bloat_.) Then ask them to think of a way to put _coat_ into a sentence. Listen to several children say their sentences out loud.

12. **Debrief.** Write the sentences on the board or transparency and call attention to capital letters and end marks.

Daily Writing Activities

1. Write sentences that use rhyming words from a list of key words like *pin* (*tin, sin, win, bin*) or *power* (*flower, glower, tower*) or *lower* (*blower, mower, rower, sower*), and so forth. These might come from words in reading and/or subject area texts.

2. Write a sentence that uses a word that rhymes with the name of a kind of fruit (*pear, bear; grape, tape*). Write a sentence that uses a word that rhymes with the name of a kind of food you eat for breakfast (*toast, boast; egg, beg; juice, loose*).

3. Write a sentence that uses a word that rhymes with the name of something in your kitchen (*blender, sender; stove, cove; sink, stink*).

4. Write a double sentence string that uses two of the words from a list of rhyming words for *bug*.

5. Write a sentence in which the main idea is something you like to do. In your sentence use a rhyming word for *tea*.

6. Write a question sentence that uses a rhyming word for *clock*.

7. Write a sentence in which there are no **Os**. In your sentence, use a word that rhymes with *stand*.

8. Write a sentence that uses a word that rhymes with a color word (*shoe-bed-bean-mellow*).

9. Write a sentence that contains a word that rhymes with what you do when you go to bed. Include the name of your home town in your sentence and be sure to use a capital letter when you write the name of your town.

10. Write a sentence that contains the name of one of your friends. Make sure there is a word in your sentence that rhymes with *cream*.

Get Writing!! Book 1 Grades 2-3   ©ECS Learning Systems, Inc., San Antonio, TX   53

Writing Sentences
with Rhyming Words

 ## Across the Curriculum

The clearest application of this activity is within the language-arts program, specifically in reading, where attention to rhyming words calls attention to patterns in the language and the relationship of sound to letter. **Writing Sentences with Rhyming Words** provides an opportunity for young readers to be young writers, as well. As teachers become increasingly aware of the writing implications of their reading program, young language learners use all their senses and language skills as learning tools.

Optional Short Lesson for Language Play

Teachers can cluster rhyming words to draw attention to various letter patterns (*rim*, *Tim*, *limb*, *him*). None of the sentences in this lesson has to make much ideational sense, although many of them will. They must be grammatically sensible, if nothing else.

1. Tell students, to think of a new rhyming word. "Think of words that rhyme with *bread*." (Examples: r*ed*, *said*, *dead*, *head*, *Jed*, *Ked*, *lead*, *led*, *Ned*, *Ted*, *wed*)

2. Write the rhyming words on the board. Tell students, "I'm going to write a sentence on the board." Write a sentence that uses several of the rhyming words.

   Example sentence: I saw Ned and Ted taking a red Ked to a lead mine.

The children will read it aloud and giggle. Then tell them, "Now you do it. Let's hear some sentences that contain lots of the rhyming words on the board."

Remember, the purpose of this lesson is to plan and manipulate language playfully.

©ECS Learning Systems, Inc., San Antonio, TX

English Language Learners

Evidence indicates that we think in our native language first and generalize what we think to new situations in a second language. Thinking with rhyming words provides young language-learners an opportunity to find language patterns—in this case sound patterns—in the new language.

Using words in sentences increases word knowledge by presenting vocabulary in the practical context of the sentence. Once the concept of rhyming is established, children will develop sufficient vocabulary to produce an example or two of their own. On the basis of what the students offer, the teacher can work to construct sentences promoting vocabulary development.

Language Activity Sheet
Writing Sentences with Rhyming Words

1. *Rail* is a rhyming word for *jail*. Think of another rhyming word for *rail* and *jail*. Make sure your rhyming word ends with the *ail* spelling pattern. Write a sentence that contains one of the three rhyming words.

    _____

    _____

2. *Bale* is a rhyming word for *pale*. Think of another rhyming word for *bale* and *pale*. Make sure your rhyming word ends with the *ale* spelling pattern. Write a sentence that contains one of the three rhyming words.

    _____

    _____

3. Think of a rhyming word for *rail* that is spelled with *ail* and has not been used on this page yet. Think of a rhyming word for *bale* that is spelled with *ale* and has not been used on this page yet, either. Write a sentence that contains one of those rhyming words.

    _____

    _____

4. Rewrite one of the sentences you wrote on this page so it is a question and needs a question mark at the end.

    _____

    _____

Writing Sentences with Rhyming Words

1. Write a rhyming word for *play*. Write another rhyming word for *play*. Write a sentence that uses one of the rhyming words you wrote in the blanks.

   _____

   _____

2. Write a sentence that contains the word *play* and one of its rhyming words.

   _____

   _____

3. Write a sentence in which the main idea is a game you play with your friends during recess at school.

   _____

   _____

4. Write a sentence that includes the name of one of your friends and one of the rhyming words for *play*.

   _____

   _____

5. Write a double sentence string that includes the word *play* and two of its rhyming words.

   _____

   _____

7 Combining Sentences to Make Meaning

—Sentence combining promotes increasingly complex and mature sentence thinking.

 ## Information for the Teacher

Sentence combining offers two advantages. The first is the thinking and rewriting. The second, a revision strategy for young writers that provides a transition from the short sentence constructions of primary children to the more mature sentences of older children.

The rewriting in this activity requires that students capture essential main ideas from two short sentences and incorporate them into the one larger sentence. Once young writers master this sentence-combining strategy, they will be ready to revise larger written pieces.

There are a variety of ways to implement sentence combining. This lesson involves rewriting two short sentences into a single sentence.

In **Combining Sentences to Make Meaning**, young writers will:

- Respond to a cue written on the board or overhead by the teacher

- Combine two short sentences into one longer sentence both orally and in print a sufficient number of times to be able to combine sentences virtually automatically

 ## Objective

Young writers will combine two short sentences into one longer sentence, both orally and in writing, and do this a sufficient number of times to be able to combine sentences automatically.

 **Tip** Make sure everyone *listens*. The *sounds* of the language reveal various ways to solve the sentence combining problem. The creativity here is in students' awareness and implementation of the variety of ways to do this.

 ## Conducting the Lesson

1. **Provide students with a cue for sentence combining.** Write a sentence on the board and ask the students to read it. Ask them to identify the main idea, (When citing examples, it can be helpful to use names of students in the classroom.)

   Example: "Class, read the sentence on the board." (**Vin ate a sandwich for lunch**.) "What do you think the main idea is?" (Vin is eating a sandwich for lunch.)

2. **Write a second sentence on the board and ask the students to read it.** Draw the students' attention to each idea presented in the two sentences. Direct them to mentally combine these two ideas into a single sentence. Ask for a volunteer to mentally read his/her sentence.

   Example: "Now, read the second sentence I have written on the board." (**He went out to play**.) "Who do you think 'he' is?" (Vin.) "You're probably right. Let's say the boy is Vin. There are two ideas in these two sentences: **Vin is having a sandwich for lunch** and **Vin is going out to play**. Can someone think of a way to write one sentence that tells us about Vin having lunch and going out to play?" (**Vin had a sandwich for lunch and then went out to play**.)

3. **Put two new small sentences on the board, and ask volunteers to put the two main ideas together into a single sentence with one main idea.** Allow several seconds for the children to read and think. (Several will volunteer immediately. Ask them to wait until you call for volunteers, so more children will have an opportunity to consider a solution to the problem.)

   Example: "Class, read these two sentences on the board." (**The car was blue. It was a pretty color**.) "Who can put the two ideas into one sentence? Tell us your idea." (**The blue car was pretty**.) "That's a good idea. Your sentence tells us the car was pretty and it was blue. Who has a different way of combining the two sentences?" (**The car was blue and it was pretty**.) "Does anybody have a third way to combine the two sentences?" (**The car was pretty and blue**.) "What terrific ideas. Is there still another way to combine those two sentences?" (**The pretty car is blue**.)

Think of a way to put these two sentences into one sentence:
Vin ate a sandwich for lunch. He went out to play.

Combining Sentences
to Make Meaning

4. **Debrief.** Debrief this portion of the lesson by drawing students' attention to the different ways they have combined main ideas from two short sentences into a single, larger sentence.

5. **Repeat Number 3 with two different sentences.** Put the sentences on the board. Ask students to mentally rearrange the ideas and combine the two sentences into one. Ask for volunteers to share their sentence combinations.

6. **Repeat with a new pair of sentences, then ask them to write their sentence combinations on paper.** Ask students to think of a way to combine them into one sentence and to write them on paper. Remind students that writers always write as well as they can all the time. Allow about 60-90 seconds. Roam around the room and answer questions as they come up. Call on readers closest by so you can see what they are reading. Listen to readers and comment as appropriate.

Ten minutes are sufficient for this instructional session. It might be useful to direct some independent practice—maybe a sentence for homework. But don't make any instructional session longer than the legitimate attention span of the average young writer.

©ECS Learning Systems, Inc., San Antonio, TX

 ## Daily Writing Activities

The following daily activities appear as pairs of simple sentences. Each pair is a daily lesson. In time, two pairs might constitute a lesson and another assigned for independent practice twice per week, until the children can write solutions to the combining problem automatically.

1. Mark was coming up the street. He was walking very slowly.

2. A bug crawled up the boy's sleeve. It was red.

3. The girls played on the same team. They played baseball.

4. Lisa stood at the door. She looked into the room.

5. The hens sat on their eggs. They clucked all day.

6. The man was old. He walked very slowly.

7. The old man looked up from his paper. He sighed and glanced down the street.

8. Two girls did their homework together. It was mathematics.

9. Leticia wanted to go to the party. She was sick and couldn't go.

10. They read the book together. It was good.

Get
Writing!!

11. He ran away. The tiger was chasing him.

12. One of the mice was black. The other one was white.

13. There were cherries on the tree. They were sweet.

14. Their car began to skid on the ice. They were very afraid.

15. It rained for a long time. It rained very hard.

16. The baseball field is big. There are seats all around the field.

17. Houses were everywhere. They were nicely painted.

18. The carpets in the house are soft. The carpets are deep.

19. The men wore buffalo robes. They were warm in the snow.

20. His skin was rough. His skin was like leather.

21. They had to be good runners. They had to play hard.

22. The little bunny hopped across the lawn. The bunny was very cute.

In response to requests for help with spelling, enforce the "three-before-me rule": Students should ask three people for help before they ask the teacher. Then if a child still needs help, write the correct spelling at the top of his/her paper and give a gentle reminder, "Now, remember, I don't give spelling words more than once." Put the word on the Word Wall, and direct the children to the Word Wall for spelling words.

Don't let spelling be a "write-stopper" in your class. Tell students that if they have to wait for more than 10 seconds for help on a word, they should spell it as well as they can and go on.

 ## Across the Curriculum

Sentence combining often demands more than simple rewriting. To combine two sentences, young writers have to understand the content of both sentences, as well as the one they rewrite. Consider the following as sample activities which combine sentences from various content areas:

1. Pennsylania is east of the Mississippi River. It is next to New Jersey.

2. Georgia is south of South Carolina. Georgia is north of Florida.

3. Arizona and New Mexico are west of Texas. The two states are south of Utah and Colorado.

Use the above sentence combining activities with a map assignment.

4. The *Challenger* is a space shuttle. It took four trips into space.

5. W.E.B. DuBois was born in Massachusetts. He lived 95 years.

6. Thomas Jefferson drafted the Declaration of Independence. He was the third president of the United States.

 ## English Language Learners

Second-language students can benefit from sentence combining by using examples from their own as well as each other's writing. For example, a fifth-grade girl wrote the following essay:

"George Washington was the very first president. He had a wife named Martha. He had false teeth and wore a wig. His face is carved on Mt. Rushmore. He died of pneumonia. He was an orphan at fifteen years old. He was ill many times as a young man. He was very shy and polite. His wife Martha was a widow. He was a good leader. He was not selfish. He was a hero in the revolutionary war. He spent a horrible winter in Valley Forge" (Peregoy and Owen, p. 95).

As an overhead projection, the girl's essay could constitute several sentence combining sessions. Students can use this revision strategy for their own papers.

Get Writing!! Book 1 Grades 2-3   ©ECS Learning Systems, Inc., San Antonio, TX   63

Combining Sentences to Make Meaning

Jorge went to the store.

Lettie went to the store.

1. Combine the two sentences to make one sentence that contains both of the ideas.

   _____

   _____

2. Write one sentence in which both Jorge and Lettie go to the store when it is raining.

   _____

   _____

3. Write one sentence in which both Lettie and Jorge go to the store to buy lettuce that their mother will chop for a taco salad.

   _____

   _____

4. Write one sentence that combines the following two sentences: **On Saturday afternoon, Lettie and Jorge went to see a movie. The movie was at the mall**.

   _____

   _____

Combining Sentences to Make Meaning

There was music coming from the lady's room.

It was piano music.

1. Write one sentence that combines the ideas in the two sentences.

   _____

   _____

2. Write one sentence that begins, **There was piano music…**, and combines the ideas from the two sentences.

   _____

   _____

3. Write one sentence that combines the ideas from the two sentences. Include what day it is in the sentence.

   _____

   _____

8 Writing Sentences with Commas in Series

—Control over mechanical conventions makes writers feel powerful and serves to enhance the communicative value of their writing.

 ## Information for the Teacher

As readers respond to their mechanical signals, young writers gain a sense of power over their writing. Second- and third-graders can develop a sense of this control by learning to write and punctuate sentences containing items in series.

Control over mechanical conventions is important, not because it pleases the teacher, but because control over mechanical conventions helps make meaning of young writers' written constructions. These five principles, written in various ways elsewhere in this book, are important in writing:

- Mechanical skill is important in learning to write well.

- Mechanical skill is progressive; it grows with practice in writing, and progressively with attention to accuracy while writing.

- Mechanical precision of his or her own written work is the writer's responsibility.

- Attention to mechanical precision is always important.

- How a young writer uses mechanical conventions is solely the writer's concern during the writing; when the writing crosses the desk to a reader, the conventions must be right.

- Writers have a responsibility to readers to ensure the mechanics are right.

 ## Objective

Young writers will write sentences that contain items in series and, as a signal to readers, use commas to separate the items.

Conducting the Lesson

Day One—

1. **Write a sentence on the board with three items listed one after the other.** Ask students to identify the number of items listed in the sentence.

   Example: [My favorite colors are red, green, and brown.]

2. **Write a second sentence on the board, and ask students to identify the number of items named in this sentence.** Draw their attention to the difference in the listing of items in the two sentences.

   Example: [My best friends are Red Brown and Ted Green.]

   "What did I do in my first sentence to separate the three colors? That's right, after these colors I put a comma. Because there is a comma after *red* and *green*, you know there are three things in my sentence. In the second sentence, the color words are not separated with commas, so you know there are only two friends."

3. **Ask students to mentally construct their own sentences with items in series.** As you write the sentence on the board, call the students' attention to the number of items, and ask where the commas should go.

Note: This is the first time the term, *items in a series,* is used. Call on a student to share his/her sentence with the class. Children are very insightful and make vocabulary transfers easily, as long as the context remains the same. Just slip in the proper terminology and carry on.

Example: [My friends are named My Luong Sam and Arthur.]

"What can I do to show everyone who reads this sentence that there are three people in the sentence?" (You should use commas.) "Yes. Now, here's the hard part—where should I put them?" (After *My Luong,* and after *Sam,* too.) "What about after *Arthur*?" (No. That's a period. You just have to put commas between the names.)

Write a sentence that includes the names of three of your friends, one after the other.

4. **Follow with two more student sentences and conduct a similar scenario on the board.** Then ask students to write new sentences with items in series. Remind them to use commas to separate the items. Students may be given the option to write their new sentences during independent time and present them as their ticket to recess.

5. **Spot-read the sentences you collect to make sure students understand the idea.** Although most students will understand, there will be several with commas spread about in disarray. Don't let that trouble you any more than numbers in disarray in multiplication trouble you. Just teach it again until students understand the convention.

Day Two—

1. **Provide students with a cue for a sentence with items in series.** Remind them that they will need to use commas again.

   Example: "Think of a sentence that contains the names of three animals you think would make good pets. Be sure the animals are in a series in your sentence."

Allow the typical 60-70 seconds for writing, and roam among students. Notice several of the young writers doing it correctly. When you solicit readers, call on them. Always use good models to get the idea off the ground, and always add good models to the list as more and more children take control of the idea.

2. **Ask for a volunteer to read his/her sentence.** Then ask the student to read the sentence saying the word "comma" every time a comma appears in the sentence. The students will find this amusing. You may have a class full of young writers laughing so hard they can't even finish reading their sentences!

   Example: "Who wants to read? Amanda, let's hear your sentence." (**The best pets are cats comma dogs comma and birds**.)

Writing that makes people laugh is, by definition, authentic.

When the students settle down enough to go on, everyone will write sentences designed to make everyone else laugh. This becomes more silly than funny very rapidly, so let it go for one or two readers, then say something like, "Let's get back to some writing we can read and listen to without falling down."

3. **Use the commas-in-series cues or prompts on page 70 for several days in a row.** Go on to something else for a week, then come back to commas in series as a whole-class activity a time or two each week with independent practice nearly every day. The independent practice should be writing single sentences in 50-60 seconds.

4. **Introduce the concept of "phrases in series."** Provide students with an example sentence and ask a volunteer to tell the class where the commas should be placed.

    Example: Maria walked down the street, looked into the store window, and bought an ice cream cone.

5. **Practice sentences with phrases in series on regular occasions for the rest of the year.** Remind young writers to use commas to separate their ideas in series just as they do to separate words in series.

6. **Debrief.** Remind students to use commas in series in their stories and reports. For the rest of the year, whenever a young writer uses items or phrases in series, reinforce the comma convention. As this becomes automatic, the children gain a sense of control, and their writing becomes better.

Tip

> Notice no procedure in this activity asks young writers to put commas in sentences written by someone else. There are no traditional "comma-in-series" worksheets. It is not that these kinds of worksheets are "bad" in some modern way, but they are about editing, and not writing.

Writing Sentences with Commas in Series

 ## Daily Writing Activities

1. Write a sentence that contains three boys' names.

2. Write a sentence that contains three girls' names.

3. Write a sentence that contains the names of three kinds of fish.

4. Write a sentence that contains the names of three kinds of animals you might find on a farm.

5. Write a sentence that contains the names of three kinds of animals you might find in the city.

6. Write a sentence that contains the names of three or more people who might come to your birthday party.

7. Think about your kitchen. Write a sentence that has the names of three or more things in your kitchen that run with electricity.

8. Write a sentence that contains the names of three or more automobiles (cars).

9. Look around the classroom. Write a sentence that contains the names of three or more things hanging on the wall.

10. Write a sentence that contains the names of no more than three of your favorite toys.

11. Think of what you like to watch on television. Write a sentence that contains the names of three of your favorite television programs.

12. Think of a way to write a sentence that contains these three characters in a series: Little girl, Old woman, Large cat.

13. Write a double sentence string in which one of the sentences contains three items in a series. (**There was a dog in the yard. He had a collar with stars, a buckle, and a name tag on it.**)

14. Write a double sentence string in which the first sentence contains three items in a series.

15. Write a double sentence string in which one of the sentences contains three items in a series. Make the main idea of the double sentence string things that are sweet to eat.

16. Write a sentence that contains three or more items in a series and ends with a question mark.

17. Write a double sentence string in which one of the sentences contains three items in a series. Make either the first sentence or the second sentence end with a question mark.

18. Write a question sentence in which there are four names of people in a series.

19. Write a sentence in which you use three or more words in series to tell about ice cream.

20. Write a sentence in which you use three or more words in a series to tell about a place you have visited.

21. Write a sentence that contains three phrases in a series. (**James went into the house, down the hall, and through the door.**)

Writing Sentences with Commas in Series

 ## Across the Curriculum

The task in this lesson is to write sentences with commas in series. Since so much of science revolves around procedure, this subject area provides an excellent opportunity to use items in series.

In a demonstration of how electricity flowing in a series can be interrupted, show five light bulbs wired in series. Explain how the current flows in an uninterrupted line through the wire and how all the bulbs go out when one bulb is loosened. As a related assignment, students write a sentence that describes this procedure by using items in series.

©ECS Learning Systems, Inc., San Antonio, TX

 ## English Language Learners

The use of English prepositions is difficult for children whose native language is not English. As writing is first an oral/auditory experience, this activity capitalizes on this oral foundation. The following is an activity using commas in a series of phrases:

Example: "Think about all the things you can see Alicia doing." [A student acts out a role the teacher planned with her earlier.] "Tell me what you see her doing, and I will write it on the board." (She's going across the room.) "What else?" (She's writing on the board. She's going to the door. She's lifting up the book.)

"Look at the list on the board: walking across the room—writing on the board—going to the door—lifting the book. Now, think of a sentence that contains two of those items."

In addition, color words, the names of people in the room, items in the room, and functions of tools can be accessible lessons on items in a series for students learning a second language.

Writing Sentences with Commas in Series

1. Write a sentence with the names of three of your friends arranged in a row, or in a series, so that the names have to be separated with commas.

    _____

    _____

2. Write a sentence that contains kinds of animals in a series.

    _____

    _____

3. Write a sentence in which the main idea is your kitchen at home, and include a series of three things you find in your kitchen.

    _____

    _____

4. Write a sentence that ends with a question mark and includes the names of three places you might like to visit on vacation.

    _____

    _____

5. Write a sentence that includes at least three things you like to do best when you play. Make sure you write them in a series.

    _____

    _____

Writing Sentences with Commas in Series

1. Read the following short sentences. (**Felicia went to the store. She bought some tomatoes. Then she came home and sliced the tomatoes for sandwiches.**) Count the number of things Felicia did and write the number in the space. _____

2. Think of a way to write a sentence that contains two of the things Felicia did and write your sentence in the space below.

   _____

   _____

3. Think of a way to write a sentence that includes three of the things Felicia did and write the new sentence in the space below.

   _____

   _____

4. Write a sentence that contains three or more of the things you do when you get up in the morning.

   _____

   _____

5. Make a list of the five best books you have read this year.

   _____   _____   _____

   _____   _____

6. Write a sentence, on another piece of paper, in which you include the names of at least three of the best books on your list.

 ©ECS Learning Systems, Inc., San Antonio, TX

9 Writing is the Reason for Spelling

—We learn to spell for the purpose of writing; spelling has no other purpose whatsoever.—The Five Real Principles of Spelling

 ## Information for the Teacher

This lesson is about learning to spell. In a writing program, the key is to teach so spelling is reinforced and progressively habituated as children write. This lesson focuses on the following "Five Real Principles of Spelling":

1. We learn to spell for the purpose of writing; spelling has no other purpose whatsoever.

2. The only words writers, young or experienced, need to spell are the words they think of when they write.

3. When writing (or "drafting"), writers must spell only well enough to be able to read to themselves what they have drafted.

4. The two fundamental spelling objectives for young writers are a) to maintain a sense of responsibility for spelling words accurately, and b) to learn useful skills for spelling accurately.

5. Words must be spelled accurately when a manuscript crosses the desk to be read by others; as long as the manuscript is on the writer's side of the desk, the spelling is in the *process* of becoming accurate.

 ## Objective

Children will focus their attention on spelling the words they think of when they write. In this and subsequent spelling lessons, young writers will take responsibility for spelling words properly.

Get Writing!! Book 1 Grades 2-3 ©ECS Learning Systems, Inc., San Antonio, TX

Conducting the Lesson

1. **At the beginning of the week, give students a cue for writing a word list, and ask them to focus on spelling the words correctly.** Pause for the writing. When students raise their hands and ask to have a word spelled, tell them to spell it as well as they can, as they will have time to check their spelling later.

   Example: "Think of something red. Put it in your head and remember it. Think of something else that is red. Now you have two red things in your head. Write one of them on your paper. Write a sentence that contains the word."

2. **List the students' words on the board, and, after allowing time for them to check their own spellings, erase the board and give them time for writing a second sentence on the same topic.**

   Example: "Now, write the second red thing on your paper. Someone tell me one of the things you have on your paper. Make sure the two words on your paper are spelled correctly by checking with my spellings on the board." [Pause, then erase the board.]

> The key is to provide students with various sources to check and correct their own spellings. Conduct a list-making session at least weekly.

3. **In response to a cue, ask students to list on their paper as many things as they can. After two minutes, call time and direct them to count the number of items they listed on their papers.** There may be as many as 10 or 12, or as few as three or four. As they share their lists with the class, write the words on the board with correct spellings. Ask the students to share ideas for checking spelling.

   Example: "Those are some good lists of words. We need to share our lists, but first we have to make sure the words are spelled correctly. If I give you a few minutes to check and correct your spelling, how will you do it?"

> Make a list of things that are long. (Think of a word that rhymes with *rat*.) Write as much as you can, as well as you can, about this word in one minute.

Writing is the Reason for Spelling

Use students' ideas for checking and correcting their spelling as springboards for discussion. While the dictionary is a good source, there are others; they can ask a neighbor or peer, see if the word is written correctly anywhere in the room, and so forth.

Tell them they may ask you for a spelling, but only after checking everywhere else, and after using the "three-before-me" rule: *Ask three other people before you ask the teacher for a spelling.*

4. **Give students several minutes to check and correct their spelling.** During this lesson, or over an extra day or two, direct the children to put words they want to remember into their own spelling dictionary as a future source for correct spellings. Select several words for the classroom Word Wall.

In the beginning, checking and correcting a whole list is too complex for some children. In these individual cases, suggest, for example, that this week (s)he check and correct one word, in a week or so increase to two, then three or four words. By the end of the year the student will be checking and correcting most or all of the words on the list.

5. **At the end of each week take a few moments and direct the children to make a "Friday List" of words they have learned to spell during the week.** The Friday List is a "spelling test" in which all of the words are spelled correctly. In time, the children pay attention to the words they learn during the week in anticipation of the Friday List.

   Example: "The piece of special paper I have put on your desks is for the Friday List. Whenever you learn how to spell a new word this week, write it on the special paper so you will remember it for the Friday List."

6. **On random days of the week conduct a variation of the "Friday List," the Alternative Spelling Test (AST).** The first time they will complain that it isn't Friday and they didn't have time to study.

   Example: "Take out one of your spelling test papers and number from one to five. These words aren't on your spelling list, so you couldn't study them. You will remember some of them from your Friday List. Ready?"

a. Write a word that rhymes with *rat*. [Students will usually laugh, as this is the strangest spelling test they have ever taken. It's also the best one, because it's the first time they have had a spelling test on the words they think of.]

b. Write a word that has two syllables.

c. Write a word you think of when you hear the wind blowing.

d. Write a "feeling" word.

e. Write a word that shows how a little girl is walking across the lawn.

Give everyone an opportunity to test themselves on words they think of to promote self- and peer-checking and correcting.

Example: "Now, I have a problem. There are 30 of you, and everyone just wrote five words, so there are 150 words to correct. I must check and correct all of the words myself, and I don't want to do that. What else can we do?" Someone will say, "We should check and correct our own papers." To this, reply, "That's a good idea. First, check and correct your own papers as well as you can. Then, get with your spelling buddy and check and correct each other's words."

7. **Conduct Power Writing once each week.** Put this chart on the board to tally their words:

	1	2	3
24 - 26			
21 - 23			
18 - 20			
15 - 17			
12 - 14			
9 - 11			
6 - 8			
3 - 5			
0 - 2			

Get Writing!! Book 1 Grades 2-3   ©ECS Learning Systems, Inc., San Antonio, TX   79

Writing is the Reason for Spelling

Round 1—

Put two words (*pony—mountain*) on the board. Students select one word as a topic for writing.

Example: "Choose one word from the two words on the board. When I say 'Go!' write as much as you can as well as you can about what that word means to you. Has everyone selected a word? Good. You have one minute. Go!" [In one minute, call time.]

"Count the number of words you wrote. Count every word and put the number in a circle at the top of your paper. Raise your hand if you wrote between zero and two words."

Count the hands and put the number in the box under Round 1. (As the children get good at this activity, increase the increments on the chart to three, then four, then, perhaps, five—but do not increase the increments beyond five.)

Round Two—

Put two new words on the board (*running—dish*).

Example: "Pick a word. You have one minute to write as much as you can as well as you can. GO!" (In one minute, tell them to stop and count their words. Ask for hands and put the numbers in the chart under Round Two.)

Round Three—

Put two words on the board (*shoes—table*). "Pick a word. In a minute, write as much as you can as well as you can on that topic." Stop in one minute. Record scores on the chart under Round Three. Draw students' attention to how the number of words they are able to write goes up with each successive round. Continue as follows:

Example: "Look at what you wrote for the second round. Put a box around what you wrote in Round Two. Now, read what you wrote for Round Two and put a circle around any word you aren't sure you spelled correctly."

If the children have highlighters, tell them to highlight the words they aren't sure they spelled correctly. Then ask them for the next several minutes to use their spelling skills and resources (three-before-me, ask your neighbor, check the Word Wall, check your own private word dictionary, check a dictionary from the bookcase) to check and correct the words they wrote.

©ECS Learning Systems, Inc., San Antonio, TX

 ## Daily Writing Activities

1. Five cues for the Alternative Spelling Test (AST):

    • a word that begins with **W**
    • a word that ends with **N**
    • a word that reminds you of happiness
    • a word that feels like strength
    • a word that has two **Ts** in it

2. List things that are flat.

3. Power Writing: *light—red, gate—talk, mayonnaise—book*

4. Five cues for AST:

    • a word you think of when you hear about a football game
    • a word you think of when someone starts to cry
    • a word you might use to show joy
    • a word that means something like quickness
    • a word that is opposite from joy

5. List round things.

6. Power Writing: *animal—eyes, telephone—father, wild—panic*

7. List things that make you happy.

8. Power Writing: *agree—fear, great—invitation, jealous—king*

9. Three cues for AST:

    • two words that remind you of a movie you saw recently
    • a word that means something similar to *thirsty*
    • two words you could use instead of *run*

10. Power Writing: *lucky—nothing, olives—grapes, fun—hurt*

    These activities will consume from a little over a month to as much as two months. To double the activities, merely replicate the schedule and put in your own ideas. The prototype schedule can continue through a school year. In every activity, students write, list, or take tests, always working with words they think of and always responsible for doing the checking and correcting. With regular attention, the responsibility for spelling properly will become increasingly habituated.

 ## Across the Curriculum

Children learn by "constructing" knowledge. In a nutshell, this means knowledge is an image and/or idea learners construct on the basis of collected information. The **Power Writing** activities described on the previous pages and below will encourage this knowledge construction.

Example: Following a social studies lesson about public officials, direct students to write *as much as they can as well as they can* about what they know about officials in their community. This kind of writing helps students integrate what they learn each day into their own system of knowledge. For five consecutive days have students write new pieces on the same topic.

Collected daily writings can be checked and corrected for spelling twice a week to monitor quality and to gain feedback for subsequent lessons. One or two students' writings can be read each week.

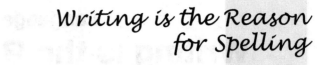

 English Language Learners

When working with children whose native language is not English, it is necessary to promote language experiences that honor learning as an on-going process toward competence. In traditional writing activities, children have been expected to "get it right"—immediately. In the spelling activities in this lesson, however, students work with their own words to develop spelling and writing competence over time.

To accomplish this, direct students to write the words they learn and the words that intrigue them; words they will want to use when they write. This kind of spelling practice gives them the opportunity to take responsibility for their own learning.

©ECS Learning Systems, Inc., San Antonio, TX

Writing is the Reason for Spelling

1. List things that come in twos.

   Put a circle around any of the things that come in twos that you think you might have spelled incorrectly. Using your spelling resources, check your words and, if necessary, correct the spelling. Write your list of things that come in twos again, this time with all of the words spelled correctly.

   _____

   _____

2. List things that come in threes.

   _____

   _____

3. Check and correct the words you wrote that lists things that come in threes. Write all of the words that name things that come in threes, this time all spelled correctly.

   _____

   _____

4. Write the words you had to correct from your lists of things that come in twos and threes.

   _____

   _____

Writing is the Reason for Spelling

1. Make a list of words that show what it feels like when you are hungry.

   _____

   _____

2. Check and correct any words on your list that you think might be spelled incorrectly.

3. Make an image in your mind of a hungry wild animal. Write a list of words that can describe this animal.

   _____

   _____

4. Check and correct the words from your list about a hungry wild animal.

5. Write a list of words that you think of when you have been playing and it is a very hot day. Write words that show how you feel.

   _____

   _____

6. Check and correct the words from your list.

7. Write the words you corrected on this Language Activity Sheet.

   _____

   _____

Get Writing!! Book 1 Grades 2-3   ©ECS Learning Systems, Inc., San Antonio, TX   85

10 Writing Sentences that Contain Nouns

—To talk about writing demands terminology specific to writing. The term "noun" is specific to writing.

 ## Information for the Teacher

There are two reasons for helping young writers understand and use the sentence parts routinely referred to as parts of speech:

1. The words we use to name parts of sentences represent some of the vocabulary of writing. Just as it is very difficult to talk about geography without terms such as *isthmus* and *peninsula*, it is very difficult to talk about writing without using terms such as *noun*, *verb*, and *modifier*.

2. When applied in the context of writing, vocabulary increases the number of ways young writers can understand how sentences work.

The key to these two basic principles is context. Young writers must learn to write with sentence parts *on purpose*, to begin to understand the terminology and use it productively.

This is not a lesson about teaching parts of speech, or grammar, or sentence diagramming—some sort of "return to the basics" lesson. It is about the craft of writing, and craft is one of the constructive elements of sentences. This writing activity uses cues and prompts to focus on the function of nouns. The idea of *noun* is best learned in this context.

This lesson does not generalize directly to everyday writing. Certainly, as young writers develop letters of invitation for a holiday party, they will not think, "Let's see, I need a noun in the fourth position of this sentence." However, when they talk with their teacher about how well a sentence works, the teacher is likely to ask, "What happens to the meaning if we put the noun here instead of here?"

 ## Objective

Young writers will think in and write in sentences under the condition that they specifically determine which noun they will use and, eventually, its position in a sentence.

 ## Conducting the Lesson

Day One—

1. **Introduce a sentence idea to the students and ask for an immediate oral response from a volunteer.** Write a student's sentence on the board and ask the student to read it.

   Example: "Think of a sentence that contains the idea of an **old man**. You don't have to use the words *old man*, but you may. Quickly now, give me a sentence." (**The old man went into the store.**) "Terrific. I'll write your sentence on the board, and you read it aloud." (**The old man went into the store.**)

2. **Erase a noun from the sentence, leaving an empty space, or "noun hole."**

3. **Have students volunteer various words that could fill the space, and list the words on the board.** The students will have many suggestions. As they call out their words, or as you call on them for raising their hands, list the words in a column that runs vertically through the sentence at the noun hole. After as many as 10 words are on the list, stop, step back, and ponder aloud their suggestions.

   Example: [Erase the word *man* from the sentence.] "Now, think of a different word that could go in the hole left in your sentence." (**Goat.**) [Write *goat* in the hole.]

4. **Demonstrate the way meaning is affected by placing a verb in the "noun hole."** Ask for a volunteer to read the sentence and to explain whether or not the sentence makes sense.

   Example: "Isn't it interesting that we can put so many words in that space in this sentence? Try this. [Write *ran* on the list.] Someone read the sentence with my word in the 'noun hole.'" (**The old ran went into the store.**) "What is the sentence about? You look confused." (**Ran** doesn't make sense.) "Why?" (You can't have a *ran*.)

 Write a sentence that contains a noun. (Specify position.)

Get Writing!! Book 1 Grades 2-3   ©ECS Learning Systems, Inc., San Antonio, TX   87

Writing Sentences that Contain Nouns

5. **Explain the role nouns play in sentences and how to identify them.**

   Example: "You have just discovered something very important. We can put lots of words in that space of the sentence, but we can't put just any word there. The sentence has to make sense. The words that must go in this space are called nouns. They usually name something, like *horse* and *goat* and *chicken* and *man* and *frog*."

6. **Ask students to write a sentence from the board on their papers, then direct them to erase a particular noun from the sentence.** Without defining the term again, ask them to give you examples of nouns, and list them on the board. Give them one minute to put their noun in the space left by the word they erased.

   Example: "Let's try it again. Write this sentence on your paper." [On the board, write: **A duck walked across the yard**.]

7. **Ask students to read their sentences and identify the nouns.** Pause long enough for a student to give an immediate answer, then give them a clue to help them identify the noun.

   Example: "The noun is the word that fits where the word *duck* fits in my sentence. We will read lots of sentences that have nouns in them, and we will get very good at writing with nouns on purpose."

With the pattern of the noun in the second position following the article, most will identify nouns correctly. Don't worry that they're not demonstrating an understanding of nouns yet. They'll have it by the end of the year.

©ECS Learning Systems, Inc., San Antonio, TX

Day Two—

1. **Ask students to think of a sentence with a noun in it and to share the sentence with the class.**

   Example: "Give me a sentence with a noun in it, and remember, when you read your sentence aloud from your head, I'm going to ask you what your noun is. You must think about that when you write your sentence in your head."

2. **Continue the oral and written processes for several days, directing students to underline the nouns in their sentences.** At this point, don't be concerned if their sentences contain more than one noun.

> *Tip* By the end of the year, second graders can write sentences with nouns on cue. There is another year yet to extend the ability to notice and manipulate nouns in a sentence.

3. **Extend the activity by calling attention to a second noun in a sentence.** Erase the noun in a prepositional phrase. As the children call out possibilities, list them through the hole just as before. Explain to them that sentences can have more than one noun.

   Example: "Look at the sentence on the board. [**The bug walked across the floor.**] What other word could we put in the space?" (*Floor, street, rug, supper dish, book*.) "All of these are the names of things, too. So if they're the names of things, what do we call them?" (Nouns!) "Yes, they're all nouns. So we have a sentence with two nouns. We can do that, you know. We can write sentences with more than one noun. Look at this."

4. **Write a sentence on the board that contains several nouns, and ask students to identify them.** Then ask them to think of a sentence with more than one noun in it.

   Example: [**Cows, pigs, chickens, and dogs live on the farm down near the river where my sister lives**.] "This is one you have to think about. Which words name things and are nouns?" (*Cows* and *pigs* and *chickens* and *dogs*.)

   "Terrific! Those are all nouns because they all fit in the noun space, and they name things. But there are still more nouns in the sentence." (*Farm*.) "Certainly. *Farm* names a place." (*Sister* names a person.) "Of course. *Sister* is a noun, too. Okay, Think of a sentence that has more than one noun in it."

Writing Sentences that Contain Nouns

 ## Daily Writing Activities

1. Think of a sentence that contains a noun.

2. Think of a sentence in which the name of an animal is used as a noun.

3. Think of a sentence that contains the name of a piece of furniture as your noun.

4. Write a sentence with a weather word as a noun.

5. Write a sentence in which the word *book* is used as a noun.

6. Write a sentence that has two nouns in it.

7. Write a sentence that has more than one noun in it, and one of the nouns must name something you eat for supper.

8. Write a sentence in which the name of a vegetable is used as a noun.

9. Write a sentence in which something you can drink is used as a noun.

10. Write a double sentence string in which you have two nouns in the first sentence and two nouns in the second sentence.

11. Write a sentence in which the first word is a noun.

12. Write a sentence in which the third word is a noun.

13. Write a sentence in which the last word is a noun.

14. Write a sentence that uses two of the following words as nouns. (*cat, Henry, desk, Philadelphia, blue*)

15. Write a sentence in which a noun follows the word *soft*.

16. Write a sentence that contains a color word followed by a noun.

    _____ green_____ _____ _____ _____

17. Write a sentence in which *rain* appears in the third position.

    _____ _____ rain _____ _____ _____

18. Write a sentence in which the word *wall* is used as a noun.

19. Write a sentence in which *light* is used as a noun.

20. Write a sentence that contains three nouns.

©ECS Learning Systems, Inc., San Antonio, TX

Across the Curriculum

Many vocabulary words are nouns. Words like *democracy, photosynthesis, parallel,* and *meridian* come to mind as typical nouns on subject area vocabulary lists. The traditional task is for students to find glossary or dictionary definitions and write sentences with these words. Without a dramatic adjustment, **Sentences Contain Nouns** lends itself to vocabulary activity sheets that can influence students to consider target words more carefully.

An assignment to use *democracy* in a sentence tends to produce a sentence like **Our country is a democracy.** More is demanded in response to the task, "Write a sentence in which a form of the word *democracy* appears in the fifth position." Now the student must plan or think about the writing (**e.g., A constitution based on democratic principles honors the majority while it protects the minority.**).

English Language Learners

It is helpful for people learning a second language to understand some of the underlying principles of the language. To do this, one must not only learn about its grammar, but its language patterns. In English syntax and parts of speech, simple sentences tend to work in an article-noun-verb-object pattern. Students can feel more confident about these language patterns when they can describe them with specific vocabulary. Thus, there is merit in helping second-language learners understand parts of sentences. In the context of writing, there is a direct connection between what students can say and write, and what they can begin to understand about the construction of syntactic structures.

Writing Sentences that Contain Nouns

1. Think of a way to complete the sentence by filling in each blank with a word that will fit into the space in the sentence.

    The _____ walked into the store.

    _____

    _____

2. Write a sentence that contains the noun you wrote in the first space.

    _____

    _____

3. Write a sentence that contains the noun you wrote in the third space.

    _____

    _____

4. Write a sentence that contains a noun in the fourth position.

    _____

    _____

Writing Sentences that Contain Nouns

1. Write a sentence in which the name of one of your friends is used as a noun.

    _____

    _____

2. Write a sentence in which the name of a kind of animal is used as a noun.

    _____

    _____

3. Write a sentence in which the name of your home town is used as a noun.

    _____

    _____

4. Write a sentence that includes two or more nouns.

    _____

    _____

Circle the nouns in the sentence that you wrote in Number 4.

11 Writing Sentences that Contain Verbs

—Experienced writers suggest that the right nouns and verbs seldom need modifiers.

 ## Information for the Teacher

Fundamental to any lesson associated with parts of sentences is the assumption that the objective includes an understanding of the roles sentence parts play. This lesson begins by describing what verbs do in sentences.

As with nouns, the basic principles of teaching parts of sentences apply to verbs:

- We need specific words to think and talk about what we are doing in the domain we are studying. *Verb* is a vocabulary word in the domain of writing.

- As young writers who already think and write in sentences begin to understand the idea of verb, they will have an additional opportunity to understand how their sentences work.

- Young writers will understand the idea of verb only as they write with verbs consciously or on purpose.

In the drafting stage, many practicing writers remove every modifier, strengthen verbs, then insert only those modifiers critical to meaning. The result is often the removal of up to two-thirds of the modifiers in the original draft. For many instructors of writing, this process is backwards. The tendency is to encourage young writers to add modifiers when they revise.

Suppose a sentence is intended to convey the image of a man headed down the street after falling from a bicycle. One writer may write:

The man walked slowly and in great pain down the street toward the clinic.

Another may write:

The man staggered toward the clinic.

From this sentence, we don't know the man was in great pain. The sentence can be written to include this information without verb modification:

In great pain from his fall, the man staggered toward the clinic.

The point is that *stagger* is a stronger verb than *walked*, and needs no modification.

This is not a grammar lesson. It is not about parts of speech for its own sake, and does not assume that since children know verbs, they will be able to write. This is a lesson about the vocabulary of writing. *Verb* is a word, an element of language construction in English useful in understanding and talking about writing.

 *Objective*

Young writers will think in and write sentences that contain specified nouns and verbs which will sometimes be assigned specified positions in sentences.

 Cue Write a sentence that contains a verb. (Specify its position.)

Writing Sentences that Contain Verbs

 Conducting the Lesson

Day One—

1. **Write a sentence on the board, erase the verb in the sentence, and ask for volunteers to suggest other words to go in the space or "verb hole."** Make a list of student suggestions in a vertical list through the space in the sentence. Explain to students that, just like nouns, the words on the list have a certain name, *verbs*, and that they tell about the action or movement in the sentence.

   Example: "Do you remember when we listed words that worked in the noun position? Verbs work just the same way, but have a different name, and do something different in the sentence. They tell about what's happening in the sentence. They tell about the action or the movement in the sentence."

    The verb space in the sentence will accommodate most "*state of being*" verbs. However, at the second/third-grade level it is sufficient to refer to them simply as *verbs*.

2. **Ask students to think of a sentence that uses a specified verb.** Describe the action implied in that particular verb, and explain how verbs show the action in a sentence.

   Example: "Think of a sentence in which *walked* is the verb." (**The girl walked home.**) "What is the girl doing in the sentence?" (She's walking home.) "What is the one word that tells what the girl is doing?" (*Walking.*) "Yes, the verb is **walking**. Look. I'm walking. Walking is my action. A verb tells about action. What are you doing right now?" (Sitting.) "Yes, you are sitting, and *sitting* is the verb in the sentence, **You are sitting**."

3. **Ask students to think of a sentence about something they know how to do.** Remind them that they will be asked to name the verb in their sentence.

    Call on a student who is likely to have a sentence ready and will be able to identify the verb correctly. Accurate models are important.

   Example: "Let's hear your sentence." (**I dance at my house.**) "What is your verb?" (*Dance?*) "Are you asking me?" (No, it's *dance*.) "Yes, it is. The sentence reads, **I dance at my house**. What is the action in the sentence?" [Everyone calls out, *Dance*.] "That's right. Think about your own sentences, and make sure you know the action so when I ask for your verb, you will give me the right word."

　　©ECS Learning Systems, Inc., San Antonio, TX

4. **Conduct an oral sentence thinking and writing activity similar to that described in 1-3 for perhaps five more minutes.** It is almost certain someone will give a sentence like, "**I play baseball**" and say the verb is *baseball*. Follow with, "Tell me how you *baseball*." (**I play first base**.) "You *play* baseball, but you don't *baseball*. In your sentence *play* is the verb because it shows action; it is something you can do."

5. **Debrief.** It will take time for the idea of verbs to settle in for everyone. In the meantime, direct students to continue to be conscious of verbs in their writing. Over time, call attention to verbs in their sentences, initiate talk about verbs, and emphasize that learning about verbs is a minor part of a far larger whole called learning to write.

Day Two—

1. **Direct students to write sentences that contain verbs.** (Any sentence they write will contain one, so they can be effective immediately.) Call attention to the verb in each sentence. Remind the class that if they use the right verb, they may not have to add any more words to their sentence.

   Example: "Class, read the sentence I have written on the board." (**It rained real hard last night**.) "Is 'pouring rain' the same as 'real hard?' Revise this sentence so the verb is *poured*, instead of *rained*." (**It poured real hard last night**.) "If you write that it *poured*, you don't need the *real hard* part any more, do you? Sometimes when we use just the right verb, we don't have to write any more."

2. **Post three new action words on the board every Tuesday and Friday for sentence writing practice.** Ask students to volunteer sentences using the verbs. Point out the way the sentence picture changes as different verbs are substituted.

   Example: [Write *walk* on the board and under it write *hike* and *stroll*.] "Think of a sentence in which *walk* is the verb. Let's hear one." (**The old lady walked in the woods**.) "Terrific! Can you change the verb in that sentence and use *hike* instead? Let's hear the sentence with *hike* as the verb instead of walk." (**The old lady hiked in the woods**.) "Try it again. This time use *stroll* as the verb." (**The old lady strolled in the woods**.) "Everyone, get a picture of what that looks like. Now, read the sentence with *hike* as the verb." (**The old lady hiked in the woods**.) "Everyone, get a picture of what that looks like. Are the ladies different? Is the action different?"

3. **Debrief.** Review with students their work with nouns and verbs. Direct young writers to write sentences with specific words as verbs perhaps twice each week. Those activities can be two-minute independent activities which they hand in as their ticket to recess. Call attention to especially interesting verbs in their reading and in their spontaneous oral language.

Writing Sentences that Contain Verbs

 Daily Writing Activities

1. Write a sentence in which the main idea is **a hawk floating in the air looking for prey**. Identify the verb in your sentence.

2. Write a sentence in which *flying* is used as the verb. (Again with *fly*. Again with *flew*.)

3. Write a sentence in which one person is talking to another person in a loud voice, but do not use the word *talk* as your verb.

4. Write a sentence in which *nail* is used as a verb. Write another sentence in which *nail* is used as a noun.

5. Write a sentence in which *hawk* is used as a noun and *dive* is used as a verb. (**Note to Teacher:** It is all right for students to change the form of words in these kinds of directions. Thus, *dive* could be *dove* or *dived*.)

6. Write a sentence in which *dress* is used as a verb. Write another sentence in which *dress* is used as a noun. Can you write a sentence in which *dress* is used twice, once as a noun and once as a verb?

7. Write a double sentence string in which the main idea is playing a game during recess. Use the word *hot* as a noun and *running* as a verb.

8. Write a sentence in which *frown* is used as a verb. Write a sentence in which *smile* is used as a verb. Write a sentence in which either *smile* or *frown* is used as a noun.

9. Write a sentence about art class. Use the word *shape* as a verb. Write another sentence in which you use *draw* as a verb. Write one in which you use *form* as a verb.

10. Read the following sentence. **An old car rambled down the street**. Think of a word you could use instead of *ramble* as the verb. Write the sentence with the different word.

11. Write a sentence in which *open* is used as the verb. Write one in which *close* is used as the verb. Write one that uses *opened* as the verb. Write one that uses *closed* as the verb. Write two more. This time use *closing* as the verb in one sentence and *opening* as the verb in the other sentence.

12. Read the following sentence. The boys were at their house. The verb is *were*. Write a sentence that contains the word *were* as the verb.

13. Write a five-word sentence in which *were* is in the third position.

    _____ _____ were _____ _____

14. Write a five word sentence in which *is* is in the third position.

_____ _____ is _____ _____

15. Write a sentence in which *was* is the verb in the second position.

_____ was _____ _____ _____

16. Write a sentence for each of the following words. Use the words as verbs in each sentence. *catch - throw - grab - toss - snatch*

17. Write a sentence for each of the following words. Use the words as verbs in each sentence. *saunter - stroll - meander - stagger*

18. Read the following sentence. *The people yelled and cheered at the game*. There are two verbs in that sentence (*yelled - cheered*). Write a sentence in which there are two verbs.

19. Write a sentence about the kitchen in which the words *bake* and *cook* are used as verbs.

20. Write a sentence in which the word *cook* is used as a noun and *bake* is used as a verb.

Writing Sentences that Contain Verbs

 ## Across the Curriculum

Precision is important in scientific writing, fiction, poetry, and autobiographical writing. Direct students to notice the kinds of verbs that appear in their textbooks and to practice writing sentences containing those verbs.

 ## English Language Learners

Context is key to learning the idiosyncrasies of any language. Learning is more likely when students have an opportunity to think and construct knowledge in the context of what they are learning.

For non-native speakers, English verbs are especially difficult because of their irregular forms and different tense endings. Thinking in, sharing orally, and writing in sentences with various verb forms encourages automatic language behavior. Such sentence thinking, sharing, and writing can be applied to "sets" of verbs such as *walk-walked-walking, run-ran-running*, and so forth. This activity should not be part of a "verb unit," but should occur for several minutes in the context of ordinary speech or everyday writing. The teacher might suggest the whole class work with sentences with the verb forms in question.

Get Writing!!

Get Writing!! Book 1 Grades 2-3   ©ECS Learning Systems, Inc., San Antonio, TX   101

Language Activity Sheet
Writing Sentences that Contain Verbs

1. Complete the sentence by putting a word in each space.

   _____ _____ _____ hit _____ _____

2. Write a sentence by putting words in the spaces.

   _____ _____ were _____ _____ _____

3. Read the following sentence. Two men stepped on the bus. Think of three different verbs that could be used in that sentence.

   _____   _____   _____

4. Write a sentence in which one of your words is used as a verb.

   _____

   _____

5. Write a six-word sentence in which the third word is a noun and the fifth word is a verb.

   _____

   _____

Get Writing!! Book 1 Grades 2-3

Writing Sentences that Contain Verbs

1. Write a sentence in which each of the words is used as a verb.

   _____ _____ _____ paint _____ _____

   _____ _____ _____ painted _____ _____

   _____ _____ _____ painting _____ _____

2. Write a double sentence string about riding your bicycle. Select two of the following words to use as verbs in your double sentence piece about riding a bicycle. (*speeding - riding - jumping - leaped*)

   _____

   _____

3. Write another sentence about riding your bicycle. This time use the word *raced* as the verb.

   _____

   _____

12 Writing Sentences that Contain Modifiers

—To "modify" means to change, to adjust, to make something better.

 ## Information for the Teacher

It isn't necessary to use the term *modifiers* to describe adverbs and adjectives, but it is the correct term. Furthermore, in any conversation about adjectives and adverbs, terms such as *modifier*, *modification*, and *modified* will be used often. The first portion of the procedures below, therefore, explores the meaning of modifier. But first, some basic principles:

- Young writers can learn how nouns and verbs are enhanced and clarified by adjectives and adverbs.

- As young writers learn how nouns and verbs are modified by adjectives and adverbs, there is an increased probability that they can modify their nouns and verbs consciously in their own writing.

- In this lesson there are no lists of adjectives and adverbs to force into artificial sentences.

In the following procedures and writing activities, young writers will:

- Learn to manage modification in order to create a meaningful effect

- Use adjectives and adverbs to enhance nouns and verbs in sentences they write under teacher direction

- Make associations between nouns and adjectives and verbs and adverbs

 ## Objective

Young writers will use adjectives and adverbs to enhance nouns and verbs in sentences they write under teacher direction. They will also make associations between nouns and adjectives and between verbs and adverbs.

 ## Conducting the Lesson

1. **Introduce the word *modify* to students.** Engage them in defining the word by relating it to their own real-life experiences. Explain that sometimes we use modifiers to make our writing clearer, stronger, or maybe more specific.

   Example: "Look at this sentence on the board. [Write: **The man went home.**] What do we know about the man?" (He went home.) "Yes, but what else?" (Nothing. It doesn't say anything else.) "You're right, it doesn't. But we could modify the word ***man*** to tell us something about him. Someone think of a word we could put in front of ***man*** in the sentence so we would know something about him." (He's sick.) "Just one word that we could put in front of the word ***man***." (*Sick*.) "Okay, so the sentence would now read. The sick man went home. Now what do you know about the man?" (He's sick.)

2. **Explain to students how modifiers work with nouns to make meaning.**

   Example: "We modified the word ***man*** with the word *sick* and made the sentence more specific. When we modify a noun, when we put a word in front of a noun to make it clearer more specific, or more powerful, we call that word an ***adjective***. An adjective modifies a noun. We're going to write lots of sentences in the next several weeks that have adjectives in them. I want you to think of ways to modify nouns in your sentences so they are clearer or more powerful."

3. **After working long enough for most of the young writers to be able to modify with adjectives on demand, conduct a similar lesson for adverbs.** Explain that they are also modifiers and enhance verbs to make them clearer or more powerful. (**Note:** In the second and third grade, don't confuse the lesson by telling students that adverbs also modify adjectives and other adverbs. At this point the objective is to write clearly by selecting the best nouns and verbs and by modifying one and/or the other where necessary and on purpose.)

   Example: "Look at this sentence on the board [Write: **The dog barked.**] What do we know about how the dog barked?" (Nothing. He just barked.) "You're right. What could we say to show how the dog barked?" (Loud. He barked loud.) "Yes, we'd say, **The dog barked loudly.**"

 Cue   Write a sentence that contains an adjective or adverb. (Specify position.)

105

Writing Sentences that Contain Modifiers

 Daily Writing Activities

1. Think of a sentence that contains the word *horse*. Think of another sentence that contains *horse* in the third position of the sentence. Put an adjective in the second position of the sentence.

2. Think of a five-word sentence in which *horse* is in the third position. Use an adjective in the second position and make the adjective give the horse a color.

3. Write a sentence in which there is a noun in the fourth position and an adjective in the third position.

4. Write a sentence that contains two adjectives.

5. Write a sentence about a girl. Use an adjective that tells something about the girl's age.

6. Write a sentence that uses *pretty* as an adjective.

7. Write a sentence that uses *crooked* as an adjective.

8. Write a sentence in which *big* is used as an adjective.

9. Write a sentence about your house. Use the best adjective you can think of that describes your house.

10. Write a sentence that contains the word *ran* as the verb. Modify the verb with an adverb.

11. Write a sentence that contains an adverb in the last position.

12. Write a five-word sentence in which an adverb is in the fifth position.

13. Write a sentence in which the word *slowly* is used as an adverb.

14. Write a sentence in which the word *never* is used as an adverb.

15. Write a sentence about lions, and use an adverb to modify the verb *roared*.

16. Write a sentence about a party, and use an adverb to modify the verb *jumped*.

17. Complete the spaces and write a sentence.

    _____ (adjective) kitten purred (adverb) _____ _____

18. Complete the spaces and write a sentence.

    _____ (adjective) man (adverb) carefully _____

19. Write a sentence that contains an adjective and an adverb.

20. Write a sentence in which an adverb describes how hard a girl worked.

©ECS Learning Systems, Inc., San Antonio, TX

 ## Across the Curriculum

It will be helpful in the early years, when young writers are beginning to learn the specific nature of modification, to call attention to modifiers in their everyday reading. In science textbooks, adverbs will caution against carelessness ("pour carefully," "tie tightly," and so forth). In literary anthologies adjectives often describe characters (*dusty*, *gray*, *gnarled*, and so forth). The more we call attention to the words and their role in aiding meaning-making, the higher the probability children will understand the words and their functions.

 ## English Language Learners

All languages use modifiers, so the idea is not foreign to children whose native language is not English. To perform the daily activities posed in this lesson, however, many children must make adjustments in their understanding of modification. Word order in English, for example, where adjectives tend to precede nouns and adverbs tend to follow verbs, does not reflect the syntactic rules of all other languages.

Writing Sentences that Contain Modifiers

1. Think of a way to complete the sentence in which *pretty* is used as an adjective.

   _____ pretty _____ _____ _____

   _____

2. Think of a way to complete the sentence in which *slowly* is used as an adverb.

   _____ _____ _____ _____ _____

   _____ slowly _____

3. Write a sentence in which you use an adjective to modify the noun *mountain*.

   _____

   _____

4. Write a sentence in which the noun *peaches* is modified with an adjective.

   _____

   _____

5. Write a six-word sentence in which an adjective appears in the third position.

   _____

   _____

Writing Sentences that Contain Modifiers

1. Think of a way to write the sentence in which **softly** is used as an adverb.

   _____ _____ _____ _____ _____

   softly.

2. Think of a way to write the sentence in which **soft** is used as an adjective.

   _____ soft _____ _____ _____

   _____

3. Write a sentence in which the main idea is something about a bicycle. Use an adjective in your sentence.

   _____

   _____

4. Write another sentence in which the main idea is something about a bicycle. Use an adverb to modify your verb.

   _____

   _____

Appendix
Organizing for Long-Term Instruction

Teaching writing is about ensuring that students become better writers by learning something every day about writing well, and then practicing what they learn. The only way to ensure that this happens is to teach attributes of good writing every day. There are attributes of good writing addressed throughout the **Get Writing!!** series. They include:

- Thinking and writing in sentences and understanding the relationships between and among main ideas in sentences
- Thinking and writing in larger main ideas and understanding the relationships between and among main sentences
- Understanding the role of main ideas in paragraphs
- Thinking and writing in a variety of genres
- Progressively mastering the discipline of conventional writing

Organizing for long-term instruction is based on these factors:

1. **Mission Statement** (see below): Create a mission statement for the year. The mission statement must be about the students' writing performance and should be shared with the students. The mission statement articulates what students will be able to do by the end of the year and how that will be measured and reported. The mission statement must involve everyone in the room and include all students, individually and collectively. It is not limited to the average child in the room.

2. **Assessment** (pp. 111-116): The teacher needs a way or ways to assess and measure writing behaviors that address the mission statement.

3. **Reporting** (p. 114): The teacher needs a way to report individual achievement of the mission statement to individual students, parents, administrators, and members of the district's governing board.

4. **Planning** (pp. 117-120): To ensure achievement of the mission, the teacher must know what both the teacher and the students will do each month, week, and day.

Sample Mission Statement

Students will be able to develop ideas and use procedures appropriate for using nouns, verbs, and modifiers in sentences to express and enhance main ideas. They will write in sufficient quantity* every school day to include these parts of sentences in response to their reading, daily journal reflections, and writing across the curriculum. The quality of student writing will increase as measured by sentence maturity, control over the conventions of standard English writing, as well as clarity and organization.

  * To ensure sufficient quantity, establish a daily general word-count criterion. For example it is reasonable to expect students to write as much as 300-450 words per day, or four to five pages. Set the baseline expectation at three pages of accumulated writing for the first two months of the year, and increase it to five pages by the end of the year. Most of the writing is practice. It must be monitored, but it does not have to be read, graded, noted with marginal messages, and sent home to be signed.

The emphasis here is on the teacher. The teacher must forge a *systematic* writing instruction program in his/her classroom without a systematic instructional program the children's writing won't be appreciably better at the end of the year than it was at the beginning.

©ECS Learning Systems, Inc., San Antonio, TX

Assessment in the Balanced Writing Program

Assessment is an integral part of all fundamental teaching. In reading assessment, we all essentially agree to look for word attack and comprehension. In mathematics assessment, we all essentially agree that we should observe numeration, operations, measurement, probability, statistics, and problem solving. But in writing, you may not agree with our ideas for assessment and we may not agree with yours. Likewise, the National Council of Teachers of English may not agree with the ideas of the *New York Times* or the Midwest Committee on Workplace Literacy, if there is such a group.

There is a serious implication here: *If no one agrees, there is no formal, relatively uniform assessment frame of reference, no relatively uniform assessment schedule or process.* The result? We all teach to whatever we determine should be the tests of writing quality, which can mean anything anyone decides it should mean. And if quality can mean anything, in practical application, it means nothing.

▶ What is Quality Writing?

List what you look for and how you assess student writing. There are only seven spaces below. That doesn't mean there are only seven items. If you need more space, continue writing on a separate sheet.

1.

2.

3.

4.

5.

6.

7.

Appendix
Assessment

 ## The Scoring System

The following list includes three items which we (your authors) look for in student writing samples. Understand however, that these are not the only measure of writing ability.

1. **Fluency,** or *How much did the child write?* Fluency can be measured by counting the words the student wrote in a specified amount of time (**x** words in **y** minutes). Fluency is not a measure of writing quality, but it's important to recognize that without fluency, a writer's chance of producing quality writing is severely compromised.

2. **Maturity,** or *What is the syntactic sophistication of the sentences the child wrote?* Maturity can be measured by dividing the number of words the child wrote by the number of sentences. We can measure maturity by counting the clauses in the writing sample and dividing the number of clauses by the number of sentences. Complexity is not, by itself, a measure of quality in writing. But as young writers develop, their ideas get more sophisticated, and they need more sophisticated and complex ways to structure their ideas in writing.

3. **Mechanical Control,** or *To what extent does the writing sample display the structure and discipline that makes written language work?* Mechanical control can be measured by counting errors in capitalization, punctuation, spelling, usage, and sentence construction. We can then total the errors and divide the total by the number of sentences.

 ## Questions and Answers

Look over the items on your list (p. 111) and on our list. Then ask yourself the following questions:

1. *Does each item lead directly and predictably to the ability to write well?*

2. *To what extent can you measure—not evaluate or judge, but quantify—the items on your lists so you can assess them again and chart progress after several weeks of instruction?*

Here are our answers to these two questions:

1. No one learns to write well without writing something. Our three assessment items lead directly and predictably to writing well because they cause the child to write something. The quality of writing is carried, to a large extent, in sentence maturity appropriate to audience and purpose. As children mature, their audience tends to mature, and their purpose tends to get more sophisticated.

2. Communication in writing depends on readers; and readers can understand what is being communicated, to a large extent, because writers make print follow certain capitalization, punctuation, spelling, usage, and sentence patterns. Thus, writing is called "good," to some extent, because it is mechanically accurate.

Each of our assessment items can be counted, thus quantified and measured again. A second assessment will show what the children learned on the three measures of writing ability.

As the writers of this book, we cannot specify what your assessment variables should be. We can, however, recommend different ways to look at assessment, such as the following, based on the analytic criteria: **fluency, maturity,** and **mechanical control.**

The First Monday Assessment

On the first Monday of the year, collect a writing sample for analytic assessment. Direct students to write a journal entry about something they learned recently, something they did that made them feel good, something they taught someone else to do, something they know how to do. Focus on this type of topic—children are experts on themselves.

Students will often ask if spelling counts. Tell them that spelling always counts: "Spell as well as you can all the time, but don't stop writing just because you don't know how to spell a word. If you come to a word you think you don't know how to spell, use enough of the right letters so you'll be able to read it later, and then make it right."

If students ask about punctuation, tell them it always counts and to always write as well as they can. Tell them also that if they come to a place where they are not sure what to do, to try their best, then make a mark at the end of the line and go back to it later and make it right. But to never stop writing just because they don't know what punctuation mark to use.

 ## *The Writing Sample*

Prepare students for assessment by making sure they have paper and pencil or pen. If your students use word processors, set them up, individually, at a keyboard and screen. Tell them that you will give them the topic, and they will write "as much as they can as well as they can." Then prompt a writing sample, getting them to think by giving them oral suggestions. **Note:** This is all oral on the teacher's part and mental on the childrens'.

Example: Mentally take them into their home. On this imaginary tour, they walk around the house and feel what it's like to be there. They look into all the rooms. They choose one room, any room, and go inside. They look around. Direct them to think about why they chose that room.

Ask them to think about what's in the room, who tends to be there, what is done there. Ask them to think about all the things they know about that room. Say, "Boys and girls, I want you to write about that room in your house. You may write in whatever way you wish, but you are to write as much as you can as well as you can. You have five minutes. [Pause a count or two.] Begin."

Nearly every child will begin to write at this prompt. The few who raise their hand for clarification can be answered simply with the direction, "Do you have a room? Choose a room in your house. Write about that room." If the child tells you that (s)he can't think of anything, simply encourage.

If a child writes nothing, that's the score for this initial assessment. This isn't unfair. If you're assessing reading and the child doesn't read, there is nothing to assess, so you wait for the next time. No effort, no behavior, or no production, is an assessment. Don't be concerned. It's the rare child who writes nothing, and we've never seen it happen twice.

Appendix
Assessment

 ## The First Week Assessment

During the first week of school, collect one more writing sample. For these first-week writing samples, give students only five minutes to write. Make sure every student has the same amount of time to write.

After collecting the first writing sample and having the children count the words, play a little sentence-writing game for a few minutes. The children enjoy it, it feels like a puzzle, and children get a sense of their own control by doing it.

"Think of a sentence that contains a weather word." (**It's raining outside, and I'm getting wet**.) After students have generated several sentences and shared them aloud, change the cue.

"Think of a five-word sentence that contains a weather word." (**Rain is good for plants**.)

Each sentence must have exactly five words. Listen to several sentences and change the cue again.

"This time, think of a five-word sentence in which a weather word is in the third position." (**It was snowing on Saturday**.)

After students generate several sentences aloud, have them write one on their paper as a Ticket to Recess. During the recess break, read their sentences and post them on the Best Effort Board. When students return from recess, direct their attention to a Best Effort Board and tell them there will be best efforts every day this year. They will be responsible for choosing and posting their best effort each day. Tell students, *"We never post anything that isn't our best effort. You must decide what your best effort is. Oh, and we will write every day so there will be best efforts each day."*

 ## Follow-Up Assessment

To determine whether the objectives related to fluency and mechanical control have been satisfied or at least approached, the teacher might conduct a five-minute writing sample on Friday of the second week.

 ## Scoring the Sample and Reporting

When students finish their writing sample, direct them to count the words they wrote and put the number in a circle at the top of their paper. When they have finished counting, direct them to count again for the sake of accuracy and put the number in another circle at the top of the page. Then collect the papers.

Using the scoring system explained below, determine the scores for each writing sample and record the results on the assessment form (p. 116), one set of scores per sheet. Conducting two writing samples takes into account that children have good days and not-so-good days. They also write better to some cues or situations than others. By writing two times under two circumstances, the average of the week's samples is a better gauge of how the children write than a single sample.

Important Note: A total of two to three hours for analytic assessment to identify baseline performance, establish instructional objectives, and show the magnitude of progress isn't unbearable—especially since this data can show the parents, the principal, the school board, and the local newspaper about how children are, in fact, learning to write quite well. Before you throw your hands up and say there isn't time in your day to do what we're suggesting here, remember that the time consumed in most assessment processes is vastly "front-loaded." If it takes an hour to do running records on ten children, the first four children consume 30 minutes, and the other six are done in the last 30 minutes. We get better with practice.

With practice, this analytic assessment system takes between 30 and 50 seconds to complete for each child. After scoring about six children, a teacher can complete each one in under one minute. That's about 30 to 40 minutes for the class. Two samples in the first week demands about 70 to 90 minutes. There will be another analytic assessment about midyear, and then again at the end of the year, with only one sample each time.

First Week Analytic Assessment: A Class Scenario

The following are very plausible average figures for a second-grade's first week of analytic assessment:

# Words:	**14**
# Sentences:	**3**
# Clauses:	**3**
Word/Snt:	**4.66**
Clauses/Snt:	**1.0**
Total Errors:	**7**
Errors/Snt:	**2.33**

In five minutes, this class writes an average of 14 words in an average of 3 essentially simple sentences. The average number of words per sentence is 5; the average number of clauses per sentence is 1. On the average, there are 7 errors per sample, or 2.3 per average sentence. Of course, there are children in the room who write more words, some who write an error-free draft, some who write compound, even complex sentences. Others will write fewer words and commit many errors. But the averages are those that appear above.

Based on these averages, the teacher establishes two objectives for the following two months:
1. Increase number of words per sentence to 20 or more
2. Decrease error rate to 1.5 or less

On Monday of the following week, the teacher might focus on Objective 16 in Book 2 (extend fluency 20% in first half year and 20% more in second half year). To that end, the teacher conducts Power Writing on Monday, Wednesday, and Thursday of the week and uses the revision portion of Power Writing on both Wednesday and Thursday. The teacher might also focus on Objectives 2, 4, and 5 (sentence writing, capital letters at the beginning of sentences, and end marks at the end of sentences). The teacher plans at least ten minutes of both oral and written attention to each of the three objectives (2, 4, and 5) on Monday, Tuesday, Wednesday, and Thursday. In addition, the teacher plans for students to write at least two autobiographical pieces between Monday and Friday (see Objective 4, Book 2).

Friday Follow-Up Assessment: To determine whether the objectives related to fluency and mechanical control have been satisfied or at least approached, the teacher might conduct a five-minute writing sample on Friday of the second week.

Writing Assessment Worksheet

Date: _____

Student Names	#Words	#Sentences	#Clauses	#Words/ Sentences	Clauses/ Sentences	Cp	Pn	Sp	SNT Errors*	E/S

Averages**_____

*Cp: Capitalization errors
Pn: Punctuation Errors
Sp: Spelling Errors
SNT: Sentence Structure Errors (Fragments, Run-ons, and Usage)
E/S: Total Errors divided by Number of Sentences Equals Errors per Sentence (E/S)

** Totals divided by number of writing samples provides a baseline for establishing a two- or three-month objective. (For example, if the the average number of words is 32, the objective may be to increase the class average by 10% in two months, 10% more in next two months, and 10% more by the end of the year.

Get Writing!! Book 1 Grades 2-3 ©ECS Learning Systems, Inc., San Antonio, TX

Sample Instruction Plans

One-Year Writing Instruction Plan

The prototype one-year plan for third grade on pages 118-119 begins with specification of genre study by the month. When a specific genre is identified for a month (September - Fiction), the elements of short story are taught and written during that month. This does not mean that September will be a month when the children merely write stories. It does mean students will write stories based on a study of story grammar (character, setting, problem, resolution) and elements (dialogue to reveal character, brevity, coherence, focus, and so forth). Such fiction study and writing appears in Objectives 5, 6, 7, 8, 9, and 13 in Book 2.

One-Month Writing Instruction Plan

A one-month instructional plan for September appears on page 120. Look at Monday of Week I. You will see the following entry: "Set up Interactive Journal #15." The Interactive Journal is a genre (Book 2); #15 corresponds to Objective 15 in Book 2's list of Objectives. On Tuesday of Week I, the second line (Sentences #1) corresponds to Objective 1 in Book 1.

You should notice several things in this one-month sample plan.

- There is both direct instruction and independent writing every day.
- There is more than one audience for every third-grader's writing.
- Students work both with genres and with craft throughout the month
- There is an assessment target for the month (fluency).
- The students will write as many as 5 stories and 13 story starts.

Given the one-year plan and one-month sample plan, you can personalize each month of writing instruction according to the one-year plan in this book, or according to a personal variation on what appears in the one-year plan.

Remember: Students must write in great quantity. They must be better writers at the end of the month than they were at the beginning *because* of what they learned from their teacher and each other and practiced on their own.

Get Writing!! Book 1 Grades 2-3   ©ECS Learning Systems, Inc., San Antonio, TX   117

Sample One-Year Writing Calendar

Month	Genres	Construction	Mechanical Control
September	• Fiction • Interactive Journal with fifth- or sixth-grade partner • Poem-a-Day	• Single sentence writing • Power Writing (w/weekly revision)	• Review of punctuation and capitalization conventions
October	• Report of Information • Each child has at least one story in process at all times; must submit at least one in Oct. • Interactive Journal • Poem-a-Day	• Single/Double sentence thinking and writing • Power Writing with revision	• Comma in compound and complex sentences • Comma to separate items in series
November	• Autobiographical Incident (three each week) • Collaborative Report of Information in Social Studies • Interactive Journal • Poem-a-Day	• Single/Double/Triple sentence thinking and writing • Power Writing with revision (twice in November)	• Reinforce prior conventions • Apostrophe in contractions
December	• Autobiographical Incident (weekly) • Reader Response to reading • Interactive Journal • Poem-a-Day	• Sentences to Paragraphs • Power Writing with revision (twice in December)	• Reinforce student responsibility for mechanical control
January	• Autobiographical Incident (weekly) • Reader Response to reading • Interactive Journal • Poem-a-Day	• Paragraph-a-Day • Power Writing with revision (twice in January)	• Apostrophe in singular possessive—if it appeares in student writing

Month			
February	• Formal Letters • Informal Letters • Reader Response to reading • Autobiographical Incident (weekly) • Fiction option • Poem-a-Day	• Two- and three-paragraph writings for transitions • Power Writing with revision (once in February)	• Pronouns as transitional devices • Responsibility for all prior conventions
March	• Opinion Essay • Formal Letter to the opinion editor of the local newspaper • Autobiographical Incident (weekly) • Choice: Reader Response, Informal Letter, Fiction • Poem-a-Day	• Sentence Combining • Power Writing with revision (once in March)	• Writing with nouns and verbs
April	• Opinion Essay • Student Choice • Poem-a-Day	• Sentence Combining Power Writing with revision (once in April)	• Writing with nouns, verbs, adjectives, adverbs
May	• Student Choice • Poem-a-Day	• Review all sentence and paragraph activities	• Writing with nouns, verbs, adjectives, adverbs
June	• Final organization and preparation of portfolio for Literacy Faire		• Application of all conventions to final revision of materials for Literacy Faire

 ©ECS Learning Systems, Inc., San Antonio, TX

Sample One-Month Calendar
September

	Monday	Tuesday	Wednesday	Thursday	Friday
Week One	• Writing Sample • Read a Poem • Set up Interactive Journal #15	• Fiction: Character #6 • Sentences #1 • Read a Poem • Capitalization (Cp) Review	• Fiction: Character #6 • Read a Poem • Punctuation (Pn) Review • Power Writing #16	• Fiction: Dialogue • Sentences #2 • Read a Poem	• Fiction: Use dialogue to reveal character in story #13 • Sentence Writing #2 • Third-graders meet with fifth- or sixth-grade partners
Week Two	• Common Story #8 • Journals to Olders • Read a Poem • Sentences #4 • Cp/Pn Reinforce	• Dialogue for Monday's • Common Story #13 • Read a Poem • Sentences #4 • Power Writing #16	• Finish Common Story • Journals from Olders • Read a Poem • Sentences #4	• New Common Story #8 • Journals to Olders • Read a Poem • Sentences #4 • Cp/Pn Reinforce	• Finish Common Story #8 • Sentences #2 or #4 • Read a Poem
Week Three	• Setting • Description #9 • Read a Poem • Journal from Olders Power Writing #16	• Describe another • Story Setting #9 • Read a Poem • Sentences #2	• Write a character into Monday's or Tuesday's Setting #6 and #9 • Read a Poem • Journal to Olders Sentences #2	• Continue Story from Wednesday • Read a Poem • Sentences #2 or #4	• Finish story • Read a Poem • Journal from Olders • Sentences #2 or #4
Week Four	• Start a Story with a Character #6 • Journal to Olders • Sentences #2 or 4	• Start a Story with a Setting #7 • Read a Poem • Cp final review	• Outline Common Story #8 • Journal from Olders • Power Writing #16	• Fiction from one of three Story Starts • Sentences #2 or #4 • Pn. final review	• Writing Sample: Score for fluency • Continue Thursday story with emphasis on dialogue

120 Get Writing!! Book 1 Grades 2-3

Bibliography

Farnan, N., D. Rocha-Hill, and L. Fearn. (1994). *We Can All Write*. San Diego: Kabyn Books.

Farnan, N., E. Goldman, and L. Fearn. (1985). *Developing Writers in Grades 7 - 12*. San Diego: Kabyn Books.

Farnan, N. and L. Fearn. (1994). "The Writing Program in Action: A Writer's Ruminations about Portfolios," *Writing Teacher*, VII, May, 26-27.

Fearn, L. (1976). "Individual Development: A Process Model in Creativity," *Journal of Creative Behavior*, 10 , 55-64.

_____. (1981). *(The First) First I Think*. San Diego: Kabyn Books.

_____. (1981). "Teaching Writing by Teaching Thinking." *Academic Therapy*, 17:173-178

Fearn, L. and K. Foster. (1979). *The Writing Kabyn*. San Diego: Kabyn Books.

Prior, J. A. (1979). "The Impact of Developmental Writing Instruction on Learning Handicapped Students." Unpublished Masters Degree Thesis, San Diego: San Diego State University.

Notes

Get Writing!! Book 1 Grades 2-3 ©ECS Learning Systems, Inc., San Antonio, TX

Notes

        123

Notes

Notes

Get Writing!! Book 1 Grades 2-3   ©ECS Learning Systems, Inc., San Antonio, TX   125

Notes

    ©ECS Learning Systems, Inc., San Antonio, TX

Reading, Writing, Thinking Gr. Pre-K–9

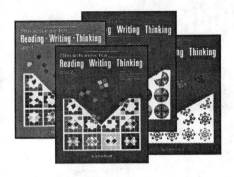

☆ Structures for Reading, Writing, Thinking
Gr. 4-9

Finally, a complete teaching program for improving students' reading, writing, and thinking skills. Each book in this series stands alone, but together they provide a comprehensive curriculum for reading, writing, and thinking in the content areas.

Book 1-Expository text structures and three types of paragraphs: sequential, enumerative, and descriptive. Book 2-Expository text structures and three types of paragraphs: compare/contrast, cause/effect, and problem/solution. Book 3-Research and report writing. Book 4-Content-area reading and writing.

ECS0549	Book 1	160 pp.	$17.95
ECS0557	Book 2	160 pp.	$17.95
ECS0565	Book 3	144 pp.	$16.95
ECS0573	Book 4	112 pp.	$14.95

☆ Writing Warm-Ups™
Writing Warm-Ups™ Two
Gr. K-6

Writing Warm-Ups™ are brief and creative writing activities for teachers who want students to make the most of every minute in the classroom. Warm-ups are quick, convenient writing exercises that encourage students to enjoy and play with words. **80 pp. each**

| ECS9072 | Writing Warm-Ups™ | $10.95 |
| ECS9455 | Writing Warm-Ups™Two | $10.95 |

☆ Best Sellers

Passageways
Creative Lessons to Improve Writing & Vocabulary Skills
Gr. 5-9

Passageways offers an enjoyable alternative to the dull, repetitive vocabulary exercises found in many textbooks. The activities challenge students to develop an enthusiasm for words while gaining a deeper understanding of language and enhancing the overall quality of written expression. Three vocabulary lists are provided for a range of reading levels. However, activities are designed so they can be used with almost any general vocabulary list. **96 pp.**

| ECS9625 | Passageways | $12.95 |

The Picture Book Companion
Books I, II, and III,
Gr. K-3

Imagine being able to create a community of readers in your classroom. *The Picture Book Companion* series is designed to do just that. Each book in this series provides reading teachers with 45 classroom-tested study guides for the best of children's picture books. Each lesson includes prereading questions, vocabulary words, postreading questions, and activities for brainstorming, creative writing, and art. **96 pp. each**

ECS9587 The Picture Book Companion, I $12.95
ECS9595 The Picture Book Companion, II $12.95
ECS9641 The Picture Book Companion, III $12.95

☆ Springboards for Reading
Gr. 3-6

These lessons serve as springboards for developing students' strategic reading skills. Each lesson addresses a particular reading skill in a "non-textbook" manner and emphasizes active student involvement through reading, discussion, cooperative learning, creative and critical thinking, and other motivating activities. The lessons focus on six important areas of understanding and skill: Vocabulary, facts and details, main idea, causal relationships, inferences, and fact/nonfact. **96 pp.**

| ECS9692 | Springboards for Reading | $11.95 |

Novel Extenders
Books 1, 2, 3, 4, Gr. 1-3
African-American Collection, Gr. 4-6
Multicultural Collection, Gr. 1-3, Gr. 4-6

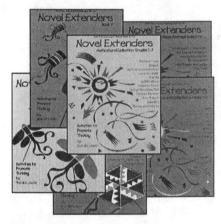

Take your children beyond the common vocabulary and simple comprehension tests when teaching popular children's literature. *Novel Extenders* include activities that will help children further explore various aspects of literature (setting, plot, story ending) in many creative, challenging ways. Each *Novel Extenders* contains activities for various children's books. Included is a cover page with book summary, recommended grade level, and suggestions to connect the book to other topics, ideas, or concepts in the curriculum. Literature selections are easy to find. **112 - 144 pp.**

ECS000X	Novel Extenders, Book 1	$15.95
ECS0018	Novel Extenders, Book 2	$16.95
ECS0069	Novel Extenders, Book 3	$15.95
ECS0077	Novel Extenders, Book 4	$15.95
ECS0506	Novel Extenders: African-American Collection,Gr. 4-6	$14.95
ECS0603	Novel Extenders: Multicultural Collection,Gr. 1-3	$14.95
ECS0786	Novel Extenders: Multicultural Collection	$14.95

To order, contact your local school supply store, or write:

ECS Learning Systems, Inc.
P.O. Box 791437
San Antonio, TX 78279-1437